REVISE BTEC TECH AWARD
Performing Arts

REVISION GUIDE

Series Consultant: Harry Smith

A note from the publisher

While the publishers have made every attempt to ensure that advice on the qualification and its assessment is accurate, the official specification and associated assessment guidance materials are the only authoritative source of information and should always be referred to for definitive guidance.

This qualification is reviewed on a regular basis and may be updated in the future. Any such updates that affect the content of this Revision Guide will be outlined at **www.pearsonfe.co.uk/BTECchanges**. The eBook version of this Revision Guide will also be updated to reflect the latest guidance as soon as possible.

For the full range of Pearson revision titles across KS2, KS3, GCSE, Functional Skills, AS/A Level and BTEC visit:
www.pearsonschools.co.uk/revise

Published by Pearson Education Limited, 80 Strand, London, WC2R ORL.

www.pearsonschoolsandfecolleges.co.uk

Copies of official specifications for all Pearson qualifications may be found on the website: qualifications.pearson.com

Text and illustrations © Pearson Education Ltd 2018
Typeset and illustrated by QBS Learning
Produced by QBS Learning
Cover illustration by Miriam Sturdee

The rights of Sally Jewers, Heidi McEntee, and Paul Webster to be identified as consultant authors of this work have been asserted by them in accordance with the Copyright, Designs and Patents Act 1988.

First published 2018

21 20 19 18
10 9 8 7 6 5 4 3 2 1

British Library Cataloguing in Publication Data
A catalogue record for this book is available from the British Library

ISBN 978 1 292 24562 1

Printed in Slovakia by Neografia

Acknowledgements
The author and publisher would like to thank the following individuals and organisations for permission to reproduce their photographs:
(key: b: bottom; c: centre; l: left; r: right; t: top)
123rf: jackf 2, Andriy Popov 9, Hongqi Zhang 27; **Alamy Stock Photo:** theatrepix 4, Pictorial Press Ltd 12, Yevgen Titov 24, Everett Collection Inc 25tr, 25bl, Geraint Lewis 38, Redsnapper 41; **Getty:** Robbie Jack/Corbis 22, Bettmann 25; **Jenny Hunt** 31; **Ken Wilson-Max** 51; **Lea Anderson** 15; **Shutterstock:** Serhii Bobyk 3, Juanan Barros Moreno 6, Africa Studio 20, 30, Alistair Muir 24l, Alexander Lukatskiy 30, Mihai Blanaru 32, Francesco Cantone 40, Andrey Petrovas 48, Creatista 49.

Notes from the publisher

1. While the publishers have made every attempt to ensure that advice on the qualification and its assessment is accurate, the official specification and associated assessment guidance materials are the only authoritative source of information and should always be referred to for definitive guidance.

Pearson examiners have not contributed to any sections in this resource relevant to examination papers for which they have responsibility.

2. Pearson has robust editorial processes, including answer and fact checks, to ensure the accuracy of the content in this publication, and every effort is made to ensure this publication is free of errors. We are, however, only human, and occasionally errors do occur. Pearson is not liable for any misunderstandings that arise as a result of errors in this publication, but it is our priority to ensure that the content is accurate. If you spot an error, please do contact us at resourcescorrections@pearson.com so we can make sure it is corrected.

Websites
Pearson Education Limited is not responsible for the content of any external internet sites. It is essential for tutors to preview each website before using it in class so as to ensure that the URL is still accurate, relevant and appropriate. We suggest that tutors bookmark useful websites and consider enabling students to access them through the school/college intranet.

Introduction

Revising Component 3 of your BTEC Tech Award

This Revision Guide has been designed to support you in preparing for the externally assessed component of your course. Component 3, Responding to a Brief, builds on the knowledge, understanding and skills developed in Components 1 and 2. For assessment, you will be given a brief and stimulus to create performance material as either a **performer** (acting, dance, musical theatre) or a **designer** (with a focus from one of the following categories: costume/make-up/masks/hair, set/props, lighting, sound). You will respond to the stimulus and create a workshop performance that communicates ideas and creative intentions to a target audience. Design students will give a presentation at the workshop performance, so their design ideas can be considered in the context of the workshop performance given by their group.

Your Revision Guide

This Revision Guide contains two types of pages, shown below.

Content pages help you revise essential content. When revising disciplines, the focus is on the skills and techniques of performers.

Skills pages help you prepare for your assessment. When revising assessment skills, the focus is on the performance disciplines. Skills pages have a coloured edge and are shaded in the table of contents.

Use the **Now try this** activities on every page to help you test your knowledge and practise the relevant skills.

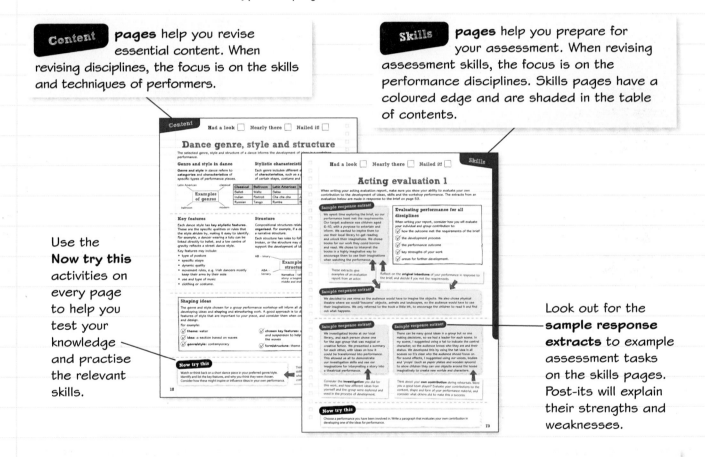

Look out for the **sample response extracts** to example assessment tasks on the skills pages. Post-its will explain their strengths and weaknesses.

Design disciplines

Refer to the specification and sample assessment material on the Pearson website for additional detail that is specific to **design** students, such as:

- **Skills and techniques of the designer**, e.g. understanding the implications of selected performance skills and techniques in relation to design, research, shaping and refining ideas, and the influence of practitioners such as Julie Taymor
- **Demonstrating during a presentation** the skills used during the development process, such as research, interpretative and collaborative skills (with performers/other designers), and the ability to communicate ideas through non-verbal media, e.g. diagrams, model boxes
- **Working effectively with others** by ensuring that designs are appropriate for the workshop performance and performers
- **Communicating ideas** through ensuring designs are realised in a workshop performance.

Details of assessment may change, so always make sure you are up to date.

Contents

1 Understanding a brief
2 Responding to stimulus
3 Target audience
4 Audience and purpose
5 Performance space and staging
6 Using performance space
7 Resources
8 Style
9 Types of stimulus
10 Theme as a starting point
11 Issues as a starting point
12 Props as a starting point
13 Setting as a starting point
14 Existing acting repertoire
15 Existing dance repertoire
16 Existing musical theatre repertoire
17 Acting genre, style and structure
18 Dance genre, style and structure
19 Musical theatre genre, style and structure
20 Skills and creative intentions
21 Working as a group
22 Influence of acting practitioners
23 Influences on acting
24 Influence of dance practitioners
25 Influences on dance
26 Influence of musical theatre practitioners
27 Influences on musical theatre
28 Skills for young audiences

29 Skills for wide audiences
30 Vocal skills
31 Voice preparation
32 Physical performance skills
33 Acting performance skills
34 Dance performance skills
35 Musical theatre performance skills
36 Acting group improvisation
37 Dance group improvisation
38 Musical theatre group improvisation
39 Developing acting style and genre
40 Developing dance style and genre
41 Developing musical theatre style and genre
42 Individual preparation
43 Group rehearsals
44 Performance skills and techniques
45 Sustaining performance
46 Preparing with others
47 Performing with others
48 Communicating ideas
49 Reflecting on process
50 Reflecting on the outcome
51 Improving process and the outcome

52 Your Component 3 set task
53 Responding to a brief
54 Ideas log notes 1
55 Ideas log notes 2
56 Skills log notes 1
57 Skills log notes 2
58 Acting ideas log 1
59 Acting ideas log 2
60 Acting skills log 1
61 Acting skills log 2
62 Dance ideas log 1
63 Dance ideas log 2
64 Dance skills log 1
65 Dance skills log 2
66 Musical theatre ideas log 1
67 Musical theatre ideas log 2
68 Musical theatre skills log 1
69 Musical theatre skills log 2
70 Preparing and performing 1
71 Preparing and performing 2
72 Workshop performance debrief
73 Acting evaluation 1
74 Acting evaluation 2
75 Dance evaluation 1
76 Dance evaluation 2
77 Musical theatre evaluation 1
78 Musical theatre evaluation 2

79 Answers

A small bit of small print
Pearson publishes Sample Assessment Material and the Specification on its website. This is the official content and this book should be used in conjunction with it. The questions in *Now try this* have been written to help you test your knowledge and skills. Remember: the real assessment may not look like this.

Understanding a brief

Performers and designers often need to respond to a given brief for performance. It is important to understand what is required in response to the brief. See also pages 52–53 for a brief in the context of assessment.

Reading a brief

A brief for a workshop performance might include a **context** and **stimulus**. For example:

This is the context → You have been asked by your local theatre to contribute to a gala afternoon. As they are celebrating 20 years since they opened, they have set the theme/stimulus for performance as:

This is the stimulus → **'New beginnings'**

They have invited local performance groups to the theatre to show a short piece of work of around 10 to 15 minutes. They suggest that each group should be no more than seven performers and no more than four designers.

Understanding requirements

In response to the theme/stimulus, a brief might require you to:

- select a specific target audience
- work as part of a small group to create a workshop performance
- participate in discussions and practical activities to shape and develop original material and ideas, and rehearse for performance
- present the performance to an invited audience, working well as part of a group to apply performance and design skills and techniques creatively, communicating chosen ideas and creative intentions for the stimulus of 'New beginnings'
- evaluate the performance.

Workshop performance

A **workshop performance** is a simple, stripped-back performance of musical theatre, a play or dance.

☑ The performers might work without production elements such as costume, lighting or set. It might be an extract of the full-length version of the work. It is used in the performing arts industry to preview the staging of a new work for an audience and understand their reaction.

☑ Performers and designers ask the audience for feedback, and also view footage of the performance to evaluate: Are the intentions and aims clear? Are changes needed for future performances?

Considering responses

Performers and designers may use a list to check against in response to the brief, as the work develops.

1 Target audience (e.g. children, elderly, families)

2 Performance space (e.g. theatre, studio, hall)

3 **Performance** (e.g. acting, dance, musical theatre) or **design** discipline (e.g. costume, make-up, masks, hair; set/props; lighting, sound)

4 Performance and design skills and strengths (e.g. individually and as a group)

5 Structure of work (e.g. short scenes, continuous piece, showcase)

6 Style and genre (e.g contemporary, tragedy, comedy)

7 Creative intentions (e.g. to raise awareness of a topic, to educate, to entertain)

8 Planning and managing resources (e.g. for development and in performance)

9 Timing (e.g. time to develop and prepare and the running time in performance)

10 Number of performers and designers (see the Pearson website for assessment requirements).

Now try this

Consider the stimulus 'New beginnings' and the context in the brief above. Think of an idea in response. Explain how it links to the brief.

The idea might be informed by existing material you have worked with, or newly developed skills.

Responding to stimulus

Responding to a brief and stimulus involves **discussion** and **practical exploration activities**.

Developing ideas

Performers and designers start the creative process by using the **stimulus** in a brief to **generate ideas** for material. When discussing, selecting and rejecting ideas, it is important to:

- work effectively as a member of a group
- respect opinions
- take turns to share your ideas
- make notes for logging and evaluating ideas.

Exploring ideas

Practical activities can be used to explore and generate ideas in response to the brief and stimulus. The skills used will vary, depending on different features:

- **Discipline** – acting, dance, musical theatre, design. Within your discipline you could use improvisation as a quick way to respond to a brief immediately. You could split the group up and improvise, then share your findings with the rest of the group.

- **Form and style** of performance – if you know the style of performance you might use, you could work in pairs to list the stylistic features you might include. Then share these with the rest of your group.

These performers are using movement to explore the stimulus of 'Stronger together or apart'.

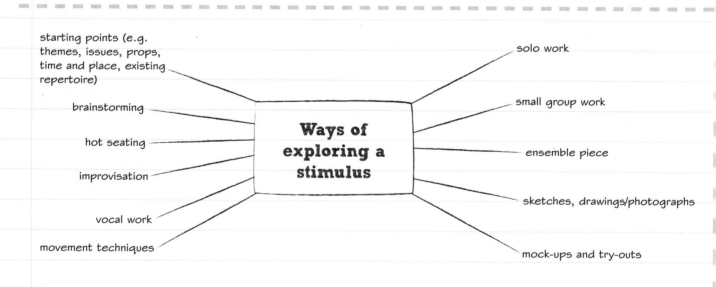

- starting points (e.g. themes, issues, props, time and place, existing repertoire)
- brainstorming
- hot seating
- improvisation
- vocal work
- movement techniques

Ways of exploring a stimulus

- solo work
- small group work
- ensemble piece
- sketches, drawings/photographs
- mock-ups and try-outs

Now try this

Using the theme 'Stronger together or apart', choose two practical activities that you could use to explore this theme in a small group. Make notes on how these activities will help to generate ideas about the theme.

Target audience

Performers and designers need to be aware of their **target audience**, both when developing ideas and in performance. There are many ways to define the target audience for a piece of performance work. Here are three examples.

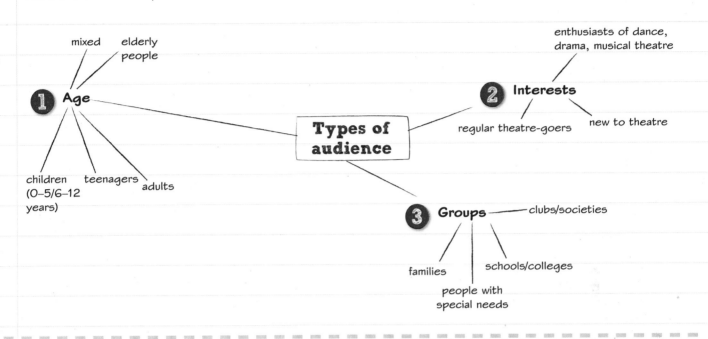

1 Age
- mixed
- elderly people
- children (0–5/6–12 years)
- teenagers
- adults

Types of audience

2 Interests
- enthusiasts of dance, drama, musical theatre
- regular theatre-goers
- new to theatre

3 Groups
- clubs/societies
- families
- people with special needs
- schools/colleges

Audience needs

There are different ways to meet the needs of different target audiences.

- Targeting adults or young children involves different language levels, ideas and designs to engage them. The message and narrative for young children needs to be very clear.
- Targeting 'the general public' is a broad audience. Specific and specialist audiences might involve more targeted needs, for example: people with learning difficulties or issues relating to health.

Define the needs of your audience carefully and be aware of any social and cultural issues.

Performances for young audiences tend to be shorter than performances for adults. A young audience may also respond better to visual or auditory stimuli than to dialogue-heavy performances.

Now try this

Take 'All of a sudden …' as your stimulus. Write down three factors to consider when targeting a performance for primary school-aged children.

Consider your target audience and:
- ideas that might appeal to them
- the purpose of your performance
- their needs
- how to keep them engaged.

Audience and purpose

The way that performers and designers target an audience might change, depending on the **purpose** of the performance. Here are **five** examples.

1 To educate
- Target audience might be children or teenagers.
- Purpose could be to cover a topic in the school curriculum – Theatre in Education (TIE) companies are a good example of performers with a brief to educate.
- Needs to communicate key points of the message in an interesting and original way, with an appropriate tone.

2 To inform
- Target audience might be parents and children.
- Purpose could be to alert audience to the dangers of fireworks prior to Bonfire Night.
- Needs to communicate facts and information so that safety is understood.

3 To entertain
- Ideas should take account of the target age of the audience, e.g. using familiar contexts or music.
- Purpose could be to entertain alone, or combine with another purpose.
- Consider the type of entertainment and any variety needed.

Purposes of performance

5 To celebrate
- Target audience might be a selected age group, or families.
- Purpose might be to celebrate a festival, landmark or personality.
- Communication should take account of religious or cultural considerations.

4 To challenge viewpoints, to provoke, to raise awareness
- Target audience might be teenagers.
- Purpose might be to raise awareness of lifestyle choices such as smoking, drinking or drugs, or consider an issue such as immigration.
- Needs to communicate the main objective clearly and ensure the material is appropriate.

Consider the purpose of a performance. For example, the book musical *South Pacific* integrates song and dance into a story that entertains, while also engaging the audience with a range of emotions and social issues such as race relations.

Now try this

Take 'Time and place' as your stimulus.
1 Choose a target audience.
2 Choose a purpose.
3 Create a spidergram with your main idea in the centre, surrounded by ideas for how you will engage your audience with your chosen purpose.

You might have more than one purpose – for example, to entertain and inform.

Performance space and staging

The type of performance space is considered early on when creating a performance. It determines how performers and designers stage a piece, and can play a big part in communicating creative intentions to an audience. Different types of staging can be used in performance spaces, for different purposes.

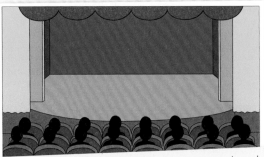

Proscenium arch, where the audience is end-on to the performance space, with one main point of view. The arch frames the action, and can be raised with a raked stage.

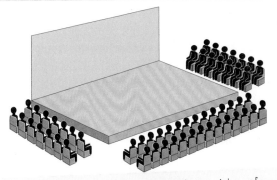

Thrust, where the audience is on three sides of the performance space. The action comes into the audience but can also be pulled back.

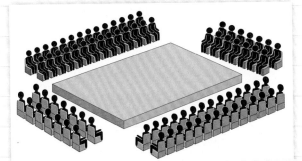

In the round, where the audience is on all sides of the performance space, which is in the middle. Performers enter and exit the stage through the audience.

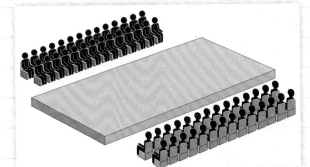

Traverse, where the audience is on either side of a rectangular, long and thin performance space. The audience is parallel and facing each other.

Promenade, where there is freedom to stage scenes in different locations. It needs confident performers and designers to encourage the audience to follow them on a journey.

Consider a performance piece that you have staged or seen. Explain the type of venue, the stage used and the reasons for the choices about the performance space.

What changes might you consider to the stage or performance space?

Using performance space

Performers and designers may need to work with requirements and constraints relating to the performance space. Using a space imaginatively can greatly enhance a performance.

Venues

Live performance can take place anywhere.

- **Theatres** – often a large stage space and auditorium, equipped with sound and lighting.
- **Community spaces** – such as community centres, schools, parks, staircases, coffee shops. Some may have a stage and others may be site-specific (e.g. a non-conventional theatre space).
- **Studios** – often part of a larger theatre, smaller in size and more flexible.
- **Arenas** – very large spaces, flexible in types of staging.
- **Flexible spaces** – performance spaces where the type of staging can be changed to suit the piece.

Staging inspires ideas

The stage space could help to **generate** ideas. For example, if there are no offstage areas, performers could be visible at all times or be hidden by set design instead of traditional wings.

A non-theatrical location such as a staircase, library or café might start a creative process. The aspects of a location could generate ideas such as an ideal space for the audience, or a feature in the location that could be used.

Ideas inspire staging

The **performance idea** could shape the staging. For example, a theme could be 'Isolation'. Performers could spread out to indicate how lonely each person feels. In a flexible space, each performer could be completely alone in their own stage spaces. The audience could move to each performer, which might lead towards a type of staging such as promenade.

Staging within staging

The **space itself** can be used in different ways.

- Different levels can help communicate ideas.
- Spaces or sections can be designated based on location, setting, character or importance.
- Think about the position of the body and the shapes it is making in the space.
- Diagrams and sketches can be used to plan use of levels, pathways and dimensions.

Choosing performance spaces

To help determine the staging for a performance piece, consider the following questions:

1 What are the possibilities for types of staging in the venue?
2 Where do you want the audience to be?
3 Where is onstage and offstage? How is this going to be clear?
4 Do you want to divide the stage space, or use staged levels to show more distinct areas?
5 Where are the entrances and exits? Are the fire exits and escape routes clear?
6 Are there any obstacles or problems within the space? Consider health and safety.

Now try this

You have been asked to create a performance on the theme 'Past, present and future'. Select a type of staging and explain how you would use it to communicate the theme.

 Use the questions above to help define the stage space in your mind.

Resources

Performers and designers need to plan and manage the resources needed for the rehearsal process and performance. This may include resources required by a performance brief.

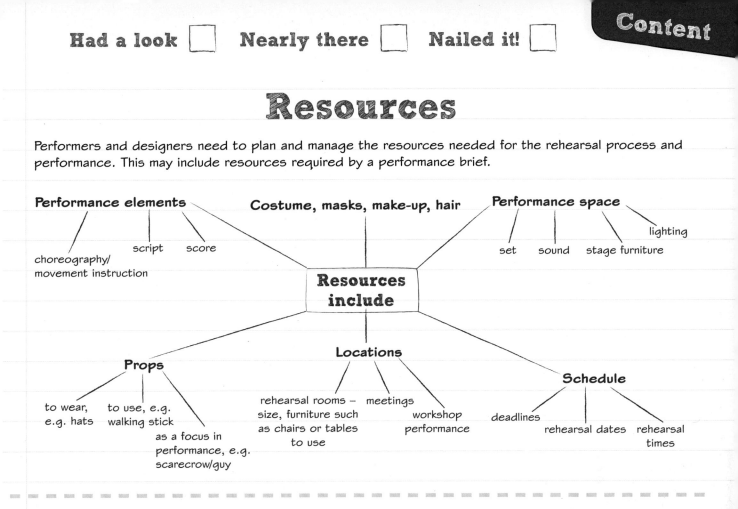

Performance elements
- choreography/ movement instruction
- script
- score

Costume, masks, make-up, hair

Performance space
- set
- sound
- stage furniture
- lighting

Resources include

Props
- to wear, e.g. hats
- to use, e.g. walking stick
- as a focus in performance, e.g. scarecrow/guy

Locations
- rehearsal rooms – size, furniture such as chairs or tables to use
- meetings
- workshop performance

Schedule
- deadlines
- rehearsal dates
- rehearsal times

Resource management

Sometimes the resources available might be basic or limited. It is still essential for performers and designers to communicate intention(s) clearly. Consider how a performance piece might be created without resources so that any additional resources enhance the piece. Useful questions to consider include:

- What do you want for the piece?
- What do you actually need?

Using resources

Solutions for basic or limited resources might include:

- ✓ making your own props
- ✓ making levels to increase performance space
- ✓ recreating or indicating objects or props through mime, physical theatre or a sound effect.

Schedules and deadlines

Setting deadlines for the rehearsal and development process for a performance helps ensure the piece is ready on time. Time constraints may be given in a brief. Some key stages for deadlines include:

1. decisions about the content of performance material
2. the date by which dialogue, songs, choreography and movement need to be learned
3. dates for design and realisation (e.g. making) of any elements such as set and props, so they are prepared and ready for the final run-through before performance
4. when the performance is to be shared with an audience
5. completing any notes, logs and reports that might be required.

Now try this

Think about some recent material that you have created and then performed, and how you managed resources. Make notes on anything you might do differently next time.

⇐ How could you improve your time management skills?

Style

The term **style** in performing arts refers to the **characteristics** of a performance piece or genre.

Style and genre

Genre is a French word that means **category** or **type**. It is used to define the overall style of a performance piece. There are many genres in performing arts, with stylistic characteristics. Here are some examples.

Acting	Dance	Musical theatre
Comedy	Classical	Operetta
Melodrama	Ballroom	Jukebox
Epic	Latin American	Book musical
Verbatim	Modern	Rock musical

Stylistic characteristics

The development of an original performance piece will be informed by the **selected performance style**, **characteristics** and **production elements**. For example:

- A West End musical is likely to use elaborate sets and costumes to create a 'feel good' atmosphere for the audience.
- A verbatim play is likely to be performed with minimal sets and costumes so that the audience is not distracted from the content and message.
- An urban dance piece may use lighting and other effects to enhance the style of the work.

Content

Content is what a performance piece **is about**. For example, a performance piece might:

- tell a story, e.g. romantic, historical
- help an audience understand an issue, e.g. social, political, age-related
- educate about a historical event
- make an audience feel sad or think, e.g. using themes such as love or conflict with genres such as comedy or tragedy.

Structure and form

The structure and form of a piece is the **way** it is presented and **how** the story is told.

- A naturalistic play or book musical typically has a linear plot. It is presented in two or more acts. Some issues may be unresolved at the end of the first act but will be resolved by the end.
- Shorter non-narrative dance pieces often have structures that resolve by the end of the piece. Sections may be given letters. In a piece with an ABA structure, the material in the first section will come back at the end of the dance.

Linear and non-linear

- ☑ A **linear** plot is one where events happen in a chronological order (the order in which they really happened).
- ☑ A **non-linear** plot moves backward and forward in time.

Influences on performance style

Guys and Dolls by Loesser, Swerling and Burrows is an example of musical theatre. The genre, style, content, structure and form influence the performance of the piece.

- **Genre** and **style**: book musical – romance, with comic elements.
- **Content**: based on stories by Damon Runyon.
- **Structure** and **form**: two acts, with song and dance numbers linked by dialogue, and instrumental sections used between acts and scenes.
- **Performance style**: naturalistic, with heightened elements in song and dance sections. Costumes and scenic elements are appropriate to the setting of 1950s New York.

Now try this

Watch or think back to a performance you know well. Use the headings on this page to create a spidergram of the characteristics of the piece.

To revise more on style, see pages 17–19 and 39–41.

Types of stimulus

Performers and designers respond to stimulus in a brief by using it as a jumping-off point for creativity and ideas. It is important to explore any type of stimulus thoroughly to inform the ideas, planning and development of a performance piece. Here are some examples.

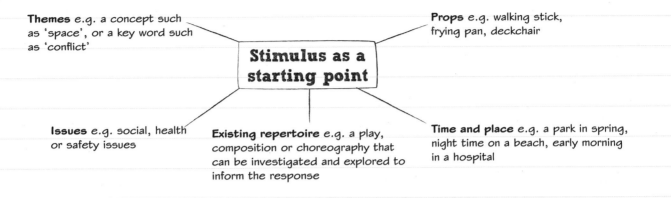

Themes e.g. a concept such as 'space', or a key word such as 'conflict'

Props e.g. walking stick, frying pan, deckchair

Stimulus as a starting point

Issues e.g. social, health or safety issues

Existing repertoire e.g. a play, composition or choreography that can be investigated and explored to inform the response

Time and place e.g. a park in spring, night time on a beach, early morning in a hospital

Choosing and combining ideas

You may find that one stimulus leads to another. You can use each stimulus as a starting point to explore. For example, an **issue** such as homelessness may lead to a cardboard box or blanket as a **prop**, and maybe a **time and place**, e.g. in a busy street at noon or at night alone. Each one can be explored as a starting point for exploration and ideas. You may then have many ideas and choices to make.

☑ You may choose one over the others.

☑ You may combine some ideas.

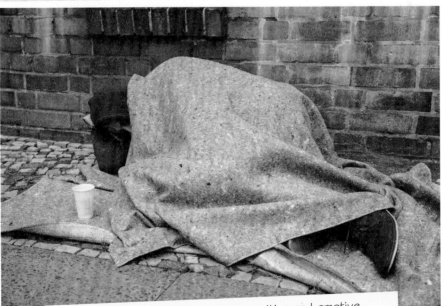

Issues such as homelessness are sensitive and emotive topics for performance.

Now try this

Using the stimulus of a **car journey at night**, consider some ideas for a performance piece for an audience of your choice.

Had a look ☐ Nearly there ☐ Nailed it! ☐

Theme as a starting point

A theme can be used as a starting point to generate ideas for performance. A theme to investigate and explore practically might be a concept such as 'distance', or a key word such as 'discovery'.

Theme as a concept

Theme as a concept could be a statement of intent, a fact, an opinion or an imagined situation and context.

- **Statement of intent** – e.g. 'Unlock your imagination' or 'Make yourself heard'.
- **Fact** – e.g. 'Death is inevitable for all living creatures' or 'Gravity keeps us grounded'.
- **Opinion, theory** or **declaration** – e.g. 'Time changes everything' or 'Performance enriches life'.
- **Imagined situation** and **context** – e.g. 'Living on the Moon', 'Robots will replace humans' or 'A world without war or conflict'.

Theme as a key word

A key word could be a noun, adjective or verb. Using a dictionary, thesaurus or thought shower can provide starting points and capture different contributions. Here are some examples of key words and their meanings.

- **Discovery** (noun): action or process of finding, uncovering, locating, or unlocking a secret or mystery.
- **Peace** (noun): freedom from disturbance, calm, quiet, stillness; a state or period when there is no war; friendship; law or order.
- **Dangerous** (adjective): able to cause harm or injury; menacing, risky, unsafe, exposed, insecure.

Linking themes to context

Context can be described as the elements that form the setting for an event, statement or idea. Here are **four** types of context to consider when responding to a theme. Performers and designers might focus on one or more, according to the theme and target audience.

1 Social

Social themes relate to society. For example:

- ✓ poverty
- ✓ education
- ✓ crime.

2 Cultural

Cultural themes relate to customs, traditions and values, such as:

- ✓ celebrations
- ✓ spirituality/religion
- ✓ tradition.

3 Ethical

Ethical themes relate to morality/what is right and wrong. For example:

- ✓ euthanasia
- ✓ abortion
- ✓ tradition.

4 Historical

Historical themes relate to past events, such as:

- ✓ First World War
- ✓ the Industrial Revolution
- ✓ the Civil Rights movement.

 Now try this

Consider the theme: 'We are all brothers and sisters.' Create a mind map to analyse this opinion. Explain how you would explore and develop it.

Thinking about the four types of context will focus your response.

Issues as a starting point

Performing arts pieces can be used to explore and raise awareness of a range of issues and topics, such as health and safety, or social issues. When working from a given stimulus, a possible starting point is considering linked issues.

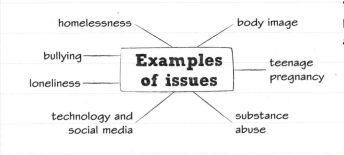

homelessness — **Examples of issues** — body image

bullying — **Examples of issues** — teenage pregnancy

loneliness — **Examples of issues**

technology and social media — substance abuse

Approaches to issues

Different approaches can be chosen when creating an issue-based performing arts piece. For example:

- in the play *Too Much Punch for Judy*, Mark Wheeller explores the issue of drink-driving and its consequences in a very **direct** way
- in the contemporary dance piece *Ghost Dances*, Christopher Bruce takes a **subtler** approach to explore political oppression in South America.

Linking with stimulus

Different approaches can be chosen when **linking issues** with **stimulus**. Some may be obvious, some less so. Here are three examples.

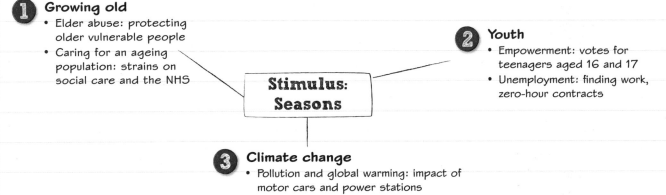

1 **Growing old**
- Elder abuse: protecting older vulnerable people
- Caring for an ageing population: strains on social care and the NHS

Stimulus: Seasons

2 **Youth**
- Empowerment: votes for teenagers aged 16 and 17
- Unemployment: finding work, zero-hour contracts

3 **Climate change**
- Pollution and global warming: impact of motor cars and power stations
- Storms and natural disasters: how floods affect families and communities

Realistic approaches

Investigating issues will help ensure that performance pieces are credible and realistic. For example, you could do the following:

- Undertake a **survey** of young people to find out their feelings on future work prospects, or **interview** someone who works in a home for elderly people. You could collect the information yourself (this is primary research).
- Read a **news story** about the aftermath of a storm, or look at **scientific data** about global warming. You could examine existing material (this is secondary research).

Developing ideas

When developing a performance piece based on an issue, use your exploration to inform ideas. For example, you could:

- use an interesting news story as the basis of your plot
- create characters based on people you have interviewed
- use the results of a survey or interesting facts to top and tail your piece through narration or the use of back projections.

Now try this

Consider the stimulus: 'Back down to earth with a bump.' Choose a linked issue and explain how you would explore and develop it.

Think about whether your approach to the issue will be direct or subtle.

Props as a starting point

A prop can be used as a starting point to practically explore themes and help generate ideas.

Using props

Props are objects used by actors in performance. They can be anything held by performers, from apples to umbrellas or dustbins. They should be used seamlessly within a production.

Gene Kelly, Michael Kidd and Dan Dailey used dustbin lids as props in 1955 MGM musical, *It's Always Fair Weather.* On their way home from a night out, they mischievously discover how effective dustbin lids are as tap shoes.

Purpose and selection of props

Props should be used meaningfully. In a production, a prop may:

- establish a character
- provide additional dimensions to explore
- enhance the mood/atmosphere
- create an environment/setting.

Performers and designers might:

- use the theme of a piece to help choose suitable props
- pick an object and see if a connection can be made to the theme.

Example of ways to use props

☑ **Theme:** 'Loss'.

☑ **Theme to prop:** use a set of keys to explore losing/finding your keys.

☑ **Prop to theme:** a cheese grater leads to how transformative loss or trauma can be.

Planning and exploring

It is important to spend time **discussing** props, but more important to **try things out** physically. For example:

- Set some rules and explore using improvisation.
- Physically explore the prop in the way it was meant to be used.
- Physically explore the prop in the way it wasn't meant to be used.
- Use ideas to set another pathway for exploring.

Practical exploration

Once you have identified props, do the following:

1 Place them in the middle of the rehearsal space. Group around them for discussion.

2 Hold and investigate each prop, thinking about what it is, what is it used for and what it feels like.

3 Identify if the prop can be practically explored (e.g. how a chair can be used in different ways) or if it inspires practical exploration (e.g. a letter might inspire an improvisation about when someone said goodbye.)

Now try this

Explore an idea for a workshop. The prop is a piece of paper and the theme is 'Loss'.

Example explorations

Theme to prop:

☑ Keys could be used to improvise drama.

☑ Roles could be a mother or carer.

☑ Idea could be panic at losing/finding keys.

☑ Progression could be to finding a missing child and the emotional impact.

☑ Research could follow into missing children.

☑ Exploration could use improvisation or interviews to create a monologue (verbatim).

Prop to theme:

☑ A cheese grater could inspire physical theatre where a group sticks together like a block of cheese, moving across a space in linear motion.

☑ Each person could experiment with a way to get 'grated off', or come away from the group.

Setting as a starting point

The setting for a performing arts piece can be used as a starting point to generate and practically explore ideas. You could consider different times and places – for example, a beach in winter, night time in a hospital, early morning in a park.

Purpose of setting

The setting of a piece is usually within the performance space and can be realistic or symbolic. It can provide the audience with visual and aural clues about the performance, such as:

1 time

2 place

3 context.

Time

When using time as a setting for a starting point, you might explore:

- **a time** of day or night when the action is taking place, e.g. midnight, early morning, 15.15 on a Friday afternoon
- **a moment** in the past, present or future
- **a period of time** in particular, e.g. the Second World War, a school year.

② Place

When using place as a setting for a starting point, you might explore:

- **a location**, e.g. indoors or outdoors, a pub, a car park, the moon
- **an unknown location**, e.g. not revealed or made clear – mysterious, symbolic
- **an environment**, e.g. busy hospital, deserted park, seagulls feeding on a rubbish dump
- **the weather**, e.g. thunderstorm, sunshine, elements of a particular season, temperature.

③ Context

When exploring the context of the setting as a starting point, you might consider:

- **the purpose** of the work, e.g. to entertain, to educate, to demonstrate specialist skills
- **the style(s)** selected for performance, e.g. jazz dance, naturalistic comedy
- **the relationship** between performers and audiences, e.g. end-on or traverse stage, audience participation
- **the performance space**, e.g. how much space is needed for performers, entrances and exits, 'offstage' areas or storage.

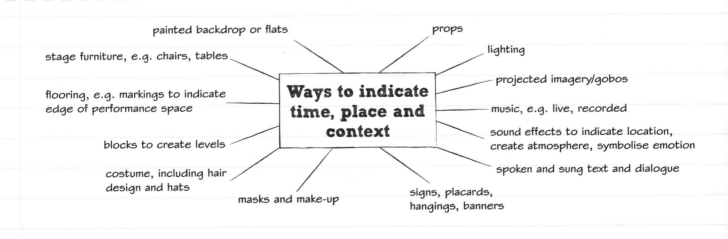

Ways to indicate time, place and context

- painted backdrop or flats
- props
- stage furniture, e.g. chairs, tables
- lighting
- flooring, e.g. markings to indicate edge of performance space
- projected imagery/gobos
- blocks to create levels
- music, e.g. live, recorded
- sound effects to indicate location, create atmosphere, symbolise emotion
- costume, including hair design and hats
- spoken and sung text and dialogue
- masks and make-up
- signs, placards, hangings, banners

Now try this

Explore setting as a starting point for an idea, related to the stimulus 'Alone'.

Experiment with representing setting in both realistic and symbolic ways.

13

Existing acting repertoire

Existing plays and productions can be used as a starting point to generate ideas for performance and design. Here are **four** ways.

1 Scripts and performance

Experiencing existing plays and productions can spark ideas.

- **Play scripts**, written by playwrights or companies, may include stage directions or guidance on interpreting the text, where you can read, analyse and perform extracts.
- **Live performances**, either amateur or professional productions, offer first-hand experience of all elements of a production.
- **Digital performances**, available by live streaming or recordings, allow you to see professional productions up close.

2 Images, reviews and biography

Understanding existing repertoire through other sources can generate ideas.

- **Images from productions** are useful for understanding elements such as props or the positions of performers in the set and space.
- **Reviews of a production** by professional critics provide summaries and notes about their interpretation.
- **Biographies** of theatre practitioners (directors, writers, performers, designers) help gain an understanding of creation and purpose.

3 Theatrical features

How existing plays and productions are broken down can inspire ideas. For example:

- **structure:** the shape and outline of the production, e.g. length of play, how it is divided into scenes or episodes
- **style:** the type of performance being used, e.g. naturalistic, Epic, physical theatre
- **form:** the specific features used in the production, e.g. narrator, flashbacks, duologue, direct address to audience
- **theatrical elements:** used to communicate ideas to an audience, e.g. props, set, sound.

4 Context

Understanding who existing works were created for, and why, can generate ideas. For example:

- **when a work was made:** year, location, country
- **how a work was created:** original play by playwright, devised by theatre company, interpretation of classical play, adaptation
- **who it was made for:** all audiences, e.g. families; particular audiences, e.g. children
- **where it was performed:** type of performance space used, town/city or tour
- **what the story was** and how it was communicated to an audience: e.g. comedy, social issue.

Willy Russell

Blood Brothers by Willy Russell is an example of an award-winning internationally successful production. There are two versions: a play with songs and a musical.

✓ **Style, structure and form:** Tragicomedy. Episodic two-act play. First scene set at the end of the story so the audience knows what happens and the story tells how it happened. A narrator is used to introduce characters, link scenes and provide background. Most characters speak dialogue to each other and characters sing, sometimes directly to the audience.

✓ **Theatrical elements:** Naturalistic costume and props. Many locations and time periods in a symbolic setting.

✓ **Context:** Written: 1983. First shown: Liverpool. Suitable for: young audiences, using pop songs for key messages, e.g. how social class, upbringing and education can impact on life choices and opportunities. Audience sympathy with main characters; ends in tragedy as objectives unmet.

Now try this

Think of a professional work you are familiar with. Make a list of its theatrical features and how they might inspire or influence your ideas.

You could include:
- style, structure, form
- theatrical elements
- context.

Existing dance repertoire

The work of professional choreographers can inspire the development of a dance piece.

Be inspired!

Performers and designers have their own preferences but can always be inspired by others' work. For example, consider:

- the skill of the dancers
- a specific moment in the choreography
- use of design, performance space or music
- communication of themes and messages.

Starting points

A professional work could be used as a starting point for ideas. Here are **three** ways:

1 Mirroring a **choreographic approach** to creating a piece or a specific dance style.
2 Creating a **design element** or **performance space** with similar production values.
3 **Approaching themes** inspired by powerful performances and communication of ideas.

① Choreographic approach

Each choreographer has a different way of working, creating very different dance pieces. You might consider these questions:

- Does the choreographer set the movement specifically, or develop ideas through collaboration?
- Do they use narrative or themes?
- What kind of structures do they use (e.g. linear, cyclic, rondo or fragmented)?
- How do they use the music? Is it closely connected, used for atmosphere or is there no connection?

Gene Kelly

Gene Kelly choreographed for musical theatre in jazz, ballet and tap styles. His choreography entertains, develops a story and shows emotion.

You could make creative decisions to use styles such as these, or learn a phrase which you could use as a starting point.

② Performance space and design

Consider professional productions that inspire you. Think about these questions:

- How is space being used, and what effect does it have?
- How are design choices and props/set being used, and how will this affect the audience?

Lea Anderson produced a site-specific work, *Car*, where the dancers moved in and around an actual car.

③ Approaches to themes

All dances have themes, whether it is the movement within it or an overall idea to be communicated. For example, Christopher Bruce used the theme of oppression in his haunting piece *Ghost Dances*, where he showed the plight of the Chilean people during a dictatorship. Merce Cunningham focused on the movement content, developing phrases and setting parameters for live improvisations or 'events'. Think about choices in relation to audience and creative intentions:

- How might a dramatic piece with a hard-hitting theme impact on an audience?
- How might a movement-based piece that explores and develops phrases communicate ideas?

Now try this

Think back to the last professional work you watched. Write a couple of sentences describing what you liked about the piece, and what you could use for inspiration for your own work.

⇦ You can get to know professional dance pieces through watching, analysing and researching them. Make choreography notes, such as what you liked or disliked, or a specific moment worth remembering.

15

Existing musical theatre repertoire

Creating and developing a musical theatre performance can be inspired and informed by existing repertoire.

Engaging with purposes

When making creative decisions for a musical theatre piece, it can be informed by how existing repertoire **engages** the audience with **different purposes**, e.g. to educate, inform, entertain, provoke, challenge viewpoints, raise awareness or celebrate.

Rodgers and Hammerstein

Rodgers and Hammerstein are examples of writers of musical theatre with **more than one purpose**. For example:

- ✓ the musical *Show Boat* was intended to entertain and also challenge viewpoints about mixed-race marriage in America in the late 19th century

- ✓ this can be seen in the song and dance numbers intended to entertain, and aspects of the plot that deal with racial segregation.

Starting points

Existing musical repertoire can inspire ideas. Here are **three** ways.

1 You might explore a particular **style and approach** of musical theatre, based on a book or a film.

2 You might investigate the way a piece of musical theatre is staged and the use of **production values**.

3 Your response to a brief and stimulus might be inspired by the professional **processes** used.

❶ Style and approach

If you are using a book as an idea for a piece of musical theatre, you might be inspired by exploring approaches to pieces such as *Oklahoma!*

- It is a **book musical**, based on the play *Green Grow the Lilacs*.

- It is an early example of a musical with songs and dances that are fully integrated into the plot, written by Rodgers and Hammerstein.

- A score and a libretto were published, from which directors and musical directors worked when creating versions of the piece.

❷ Production values and setting

Consider what you could take from investigating professional productions that engage you. For example, *The Lion King* is an example of musical theatre **developed from a film** animated by Disney.

- It was developed for stage by director Judy Taymor, using the plot and songs from the film as well as additional songs and scenes.

- The piece uses 'humanimals', large hollow puppets that allow the audience to see the puppeteer.

- Dance also features heavily in the musical, and the choreography includes elements of traditional African dance styles.

❸ Using processes

The processes used to develop a piece of existing repertoire may inspire your approach. For example:

- **responding to stimuli to generate ideas** such as books, historic events, cartoons or songs

- **exploring and developing ideas** for ways to bring the show to life in the performance space, during rehearsals

- **teaching material to performers** led by the choreographer/musical director, to learn songs quickly and accurately. In a sitzprobe, seated performers sing with the orchestra for the first time, focusing on integrating performance

- **refining and adjusting material** to make improvements. Many professional shows have preview performances which can inspire ideas to improve the piece.

Now try this

Think back to watching a professional work that engaged and inspired you. Write a couple of sentences describing what you liked about the piece, and what you might use for inspiration or to influence your own creative work.

Acting genre, style and structure

The development of ideas for acting in a workshop performance is informed by the chosen genre, style and structure of the piece.

Acting genre and style

Genre and **style** in acting refer to **categories** and **characteristics** of specific types of performance pieces. Examples include comedy, tragedy, docudrama, history play, political play, physical theatre and Theatre in Education (TIE).

Mixing genre and style

Many plays and performance texts cross more than one genre and stylistic characteristic, such as political farce, tragicomedy or comic thriller.

Stylistic characteristics

Each genre includes different **acting styles** with a set of **characteristics**. Examples are a particular form, how a character is interpreted or how a work is staged (e.g. setting, dialogue, movement).

Genre	Characteristic and form
Comedy	Farce, black comedy, romantic, satire
Tragedy	Melodrama, mystery, thriller, social drama
History play	Shakespeare's history plays, Epic, morality
TIE	Verbatim, forum theatre, Epic

Key features

Each acting style has **key stylistic features**. For example, actors don't talk directly to the audience in a naturalistic play, and don't rely on spoken text to communicate ideas in physical theatre. Contemporary plays may include features from more than one acting style.

Key stylistic features may include:

- **type of acting** – e.g. naturalism (realism), non-naturalism (stylised). For example, romantic naturalistic comedy; non-naturalistic history play; verbatim, TIE social drama
- **relationship with audience** – e.g. fourth wall 'naturalism' (like the audience are watching through a glass wall), direct audience address (as seen in pantomime)
- **plot/story/treatment of themes** – e.g. a journey, a conflict, a romance, a social issue
- **structure of the play** – e.g. episodic short scenes, three or five acts
- **structure and form of each scene** – e.g. ensemble scene, duologue, narrator linking scenes
- **use of production elements** – e.g. staging, set, lighting, sound/music
- **interpretation of character** – e.g. costume, props, make-up, masks.

Shaping ideas

The genre and style chosen for a group performance workshop will inform all decisions when developing ideas and **shaping** and **structuring** work. A good approach is to decide on the key features of style that are important to your piece and consider them when creating the elements of your performance.

For example:

- ✓ **theme:** same old mistakes
- ✓ **idea:** three generations of a family dealing with love and loss, with the same behaviours repeated
- ✓ **genre/style:** tragicomedy – text-based naturalistic and non-naturalistic physical theatre
- ✓ **chosen key features:** symbolic setting, realistic dialogue, fourth wall
- ✓ **form/structure:** episodic naturalistic scenes linked by physical movement sequences.

Now try this

Watch or think back on an extract from a play in your preferred genre/style. List the key features and how they are used in the piece. Consider how these might inspire or influence ideas in your own performance.

Think about how you can put to best use your performance skills and those of your group, what your theme is and what you may be communicating.

Dance genre, style and structure

The selected genre, style and structure of a dance informs the development of ideas in a workshop performance.

Genre and style in dance

Genre and style in dance refers to **categories** and **characteristics** of specific types of performance pieces.

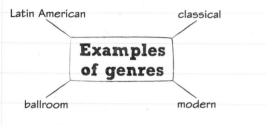

Latin American

classical

Examples of genres

ballroom

modern

Stylistic characteristics

Each genre includes different **dance styles** with a set of **characteristics**, such as a particular energy and use of certain steps, design, costume and music.

Classical	Ballroom	Latin American	Modern
Ballet	Waltz	Salsa	Contemporary
Indian	Foxtrot	Cha cha cha	Jazz
Russian	Tango	Rumba	Street

Key features

Each dance style has **key stylistic features**. These are the specific qualities or rules that the style abides by, making it easy to identify. For example, a dancer wearing a tutu can be linked directly to ballet, and a low centre of gravity reflects a street dance style.

Key features may include:

- type of posture
- specific steps
- dynamic quality
- movement rules, e.g. Irish dancers mostly keep their arms by their side
- use and type of music
- clothing or costume.

Structure

Compositional structures relate to how dance is **organised**. For example, if a dance tells a story, it has a narrative structure.

Each structure has rules to follow. Some rules may be broken, or the structure may change completely to support the development of ideas.

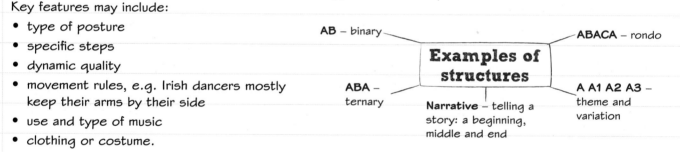

AB – binary

ABACA – rondo

Examples of structures

ABA – ternary

Narrative – telling a story: a beginning, middle and end

A A1 A2 A3 – theme and variation

Shaping ideas

The genre and style chosen for a group performance workshop will inform all decisions when developing ideas and **shaping** and **structuring** work. A good approach is to decide on the key features of style that are important to your piece, and consider them when creating your movement and design. For example:

- ✓ **theme:** water
- ✓ **idea:** a section based on waves
- ✓ **genre/style:** contemporary

- ✓ **chosen key features:** use of floor work, fall and suspension to help create the motion of the waves
- ✓ **form/structure:** theme and variation.

Now try this

Watch or think back on a short dance piece in your preferred genre/style. Identify and list the key features, and why you think they were chosen. Consider how these might inspire or influence ideas in your own performance and design.

> Think about the performance and design skills of your group, and what you might wish to communicate in a dance.

Musical theatre genre, style and structure

The development of ideas for a workshop performance is informed by the selected genre, style and structure of the musical theatre piece.

Genre and style in musical theatre

Genre and **style** in musical theatre refer to **categories** and **characteristics** of specific types of performance pieces. Popular music theatre examples include:

- book musicals, e.g. *Oklahoma!, Guys and Dolls*
- operetta, e.g. *The Pirates of Penzance, The Merry Widow*
- jukebox musical, e.g. *Mamma Mia, We Will Rock You*
- rock musical, e.g. *Hair, Hamilton*.

Key features

Each musical theatre genre has **key stylistic features**. These are specific to the genre and make it easy to identify.

Genre	Stylistic feature
Jukebox musical	Existing songs from pop band or artist
20th century book musicals	Male/female juvenile lead characters

Some contemporary musicals include features from more than one genre. Key stylistic features may include:

- **style of music and singing** – e.g. pop, rock, light opera
- **style of dance** – e.g. jazz, ballet
- **themes** – e.g. forbidden love, conflict, historical
- **plot/story** – e.g. romance, adventure, mystery
- **character types** – e.g. juvenile lead, comic character, villain
- **use of production elements** – e.g. costume, set, lighting.

Common elements

Musical theatre combines three elements:

1. **Music/songs**, including solos, duets, chorus numbers and instrumental sections.

2. **Dance sequences** within songs or as separate elements, such as interludes.

3. **Libretto** – sections of spoken dialogue. In some musicals, libretto is replaced with 'sung through' elements of dialogue.

Functions

Music and **dance** can be used to set or change the mood, heighten drama or emotion and provide an interlude.

Dialogue and **song** can be used for plot development and character and relationship development.

Shaping ideas

The chosen genre and style for a workshop performance will inform all decisions when developing, **shaping** and **structuring** work. It is good to decide on the key features and elements that are important to your piece. For example:

- ✓ **theme:** finding love again
- ✓ **idea:** three couples meet in the same locations at different times in history
- ✓ **genre/style:** jukebox musical
- ✓ **chosen elements:** songs by Ariana Grande, dialogue and dance
- ✓ **form/structure:** three scenes include song/dialogue, linked by dance interludes.

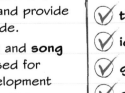

Now try this

Watch or think back on extracts from musicals in your preferred genre/style. List the key features and how they are used in the piece. Consider how these might inspire or influence ideas in your own performance and design.

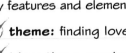

Think about the performance and design skills of your group, and how you can put them to best use.

Skills and creative intentions

The development of ideas for a performance is informed by the skills of the performers and designers, and their creative intentions.

Linking skills and ideas

Knowing the **skills**, **knowledge** and **expertise** of members of a group can inform ideas and help decide who does what.

- If a group is particularly good at contemporary dance or Epic theatre, this might influence the selected style.
- If someone has sheet music and someone else can play an instrument, you could include a song and have live music.
- If someone writes quickly, they might take notes of meetings, ideas and decisions.
- If someone knows how to edit music or scripts, they might organise these resources.

This dance piece in response to the theme 'Celebrate' used the skills of group members who could perform gymnastic dance moves.

Identifying skills and knowledge

At the start of the creative process, write down the skills and knowledge of the group. Start with your own list and then share it so that others might identify a skill you haven't noted. For example:

- I am good at choreography.
- I can play the piano.
- I have good stamina.
- I am particularly good at contemporary dance.
- I am expressive with my body.
- I can sing and dance at the same time.
- I can project my voice well.
- I know how to edit music.
- I am not scared to be a silly character.
- I have lots of sheet music at home.
- I can take notes and type quickly.
- I know how to do lifts safely.
- I know how to warm up the voice properly.
- I can develop my design skills.

Creative intentions

Creative intention relates to what you are trying to **express** or **communicate** in performance. This could be a serious topic, or might be purely for entertainment. When making and explaining a creative decision, make sure you can support it by stating why you made that choice. As you select creative ideas, answer these questions:

- How effective is this idea? Will it work?
- To what extent does the group have the skills and techniques to contribute to the performance successfully?

Developing ideas

Your creative intention will help you make decisions as you develop your work.

Creative intention

To communicate how mental health affects teenagers.

Scenes

1 Bullying scene.
2 Statistics scene.
3 Bipolar physical theatre sequence.
4 Depression split-stage scene.

Need to develop Scene 1 to make the link clear to mental health. Are they bullied because of a mental health issue, or does the issue cause the bullying? Workshop this next week to create the link.

Now try this

Create a list of your own skills and knowledge you could bring to a performance.

Think about the activities you take part in, inside and outside school. Ask someone who knows you well if they can add anything.

Working as a group

When developing ideas and responding to a brief through discussion and practical exploration activities, performers and designers need strategies to work effectively as a group. Here are **four ways** to make individual contributions and respond to the contributions of others.

1 Individual contributions

Ideas should be shared clearly so the group understands them.

- Be brave and imaginative with ideas.
- Jot ideas down so you remember them.
- Check that the ideas meet the requirements of the brief.
- Be concise and clear.
- Make sure your ideas are understood.

2 Responding to contributions of others

Everyone in a performance group should contribute ideas. You could, for example:

- take it in turns to suggest ideas, holding an agreed object to show that you are speaking and no one can interrupt
- write down ideas anonymously, with contributions from each member then picked randomly from a hat and given equal time for consideration
- discuss the ideas and ways they might be developed, making sure that each person contributes.

3 Reliability

Every member of the group should be relied on to be:

- **prepared**: be ready to lead or follow a warm-up at the start of the rehearsal
- **punctual**: arrive on time, having learned lines and movements
- **consistent**: set a high standard from the start and don't let it drop
- **committed**: so the group can develop work properly
- **timely**: meet your deadlines
- **non-judgemental**: accepting and open to thinking through everyone's ideas
- **positive**: so that working together is safe, happy and productive.

4 Supporting others

Every member of the group should support each other to be:

- **trusting**: make sure that you trust your group members when rehearsing and performing in close physical proximity
- **supportive**: if you are providing feedback to someone else's idea, be as constructive and sensitive as possible
- **listening**: if it helps, write down instructions and feedback
- **respectful**: make sure you respect others' opinions and skills – if you think something could be done differently, suggest an alternative idea or approach.

Now try this

Consider your own strengths and areas for development in relation to:
- how you contribute to the exploration or development of ideas
- your individual contribution to the rehearsal process
- key strengths of your work.

List any problems you are encountering and what you can do to solve them.

When keeping an ideas log, keep track of contributions by preparing in advance and making regular notes after sessions. See pages 54–55 to revise what is needed for your ideas log.

Influence of acting practitioners

Performance and design can be influenced by the **skills and techniques of experienced practitioners**. Pages 22–27 provide examples for acting, dance and musical theatre, including Brecht and Fosse.

Bertolt Brecht

Bertolt Brecht was an influential playwright and director. He is known for his work in developing **Epic theatre**, for example. This is a style of performance aimed at **instructing and educating** an audience, as well as entertaining them.

Brecht was a medical orderly in the First World War, and was horrified by the effects of war. His play *Mother Courage and Her Children* is set in Europe during the Thirty Years' War. Brecht used a distancing effect to separate the audience from the action so they engaged in the issues as critical observers.

Non-naturalistic style

Brecht wanted theatre to bring about change, so his work in developing the style of Epic theatre was to be **non-naturalistic**.

Naturalistic theatre	Non-naturalistic theatre
Audience believes the action on stage and feels emotion through the events happening, as if in real life.	Audience is reminded they are watching theatre, not real life, through a range of devices.
Audience is emotionally involved in characters.	Audience is objective and distant from characters.
Audience can lose the ability to think and judge.	Audience makes rational judgements about social comment and issues.

Verfremdungseffekt

Brecht used the term **Verfremdungseffekt** for the act of **distancing** the audience from emotional involvement. This technique can be effective in performance to focus the audience on a **social**, **moral** or **political message**.

Puts a social or political message at the centre.

Message must be clear to the audience and more important than character.

Form and style ensures the audience is aware, objective, thinks and reasons.

The drama can be divided up to cover many years in episodes, not always in sequential order – episodes can stand alone.

Epic theatre

Can be used to examine social conditions, inequalities, morals and ethics.

Action is determined by context and conditions – such as 'good' people (law-abiding, compassionate) forced to do 'bad' things (break the law, make tough decisions) to survive.

Can be used to educate and enable change in society – humans and society are not fixed, and can be changed.

Now try this

Select a key practitioner you are interested in or have studied. Make notes on their style of performance and the key stylistic features of their work.

You could discover other practitioners who use verbatim theatre, and make comparisons between the style and content of their work.

Influences on acting

Influential playwrights can inform the way performers and designers use **skills and techniques** to realise creative ideas in response to a brief for a workshop performance.

Style and form

A performance influenced by Brecht's Epic theatre might create meaning through the following techniques:

- **Distancing**, shattering the illusion that it is real – e.g. highlighting the artificial, making the familiar unfamiliar and vice versa, interrupting the narrative and fluidity of production.
- **Using narrative** to tell a detached story to explore humans in a particular social or political context. Signs, placards and projections could provide context, e.g. date, location, what happens next.
- **Using a summary of a scene** before it begins – it's not about *what* happens but *why* it happens.
- **Using episodes and standalone scenes** that can span different years and locations, with songs and cabaret to break up the action.
- Using **humour**, **comedy** and **fun** ('Spass') so the audience enjoys the work in order to think and learn from it.
- **Using gesture and attitude** to create clarity of creative intent.
- **Working with an audience** through direct address, or asking them questions while a scene is taking place.

Characters

Using Brecht's techniques might influence skills and techniques used with characters:

- **Create central 'real'/'good' characters** that are recognisable and lifelike, so the audience can know and understand them.
- **Create 'baddies'** who are extreme stereotypes or caricatures so the message is clear.
- **Demonstrate and present a character** to an audience, and step out of character, rather than 'being' that character. Character names can reflect status and social type. A character can talk about themselves in the third person to distance the emotion of a scene.
- **Have moral choices** for central characters to decide upon. Every person has free will, not a predetermined path in life.
- **Have fun** to ridicule a character, situation or system in order to engage the audience and expose faults.

Fourth wall

Epic theatre breaks the **imaginary wall** between the audience and the actors. The audience does not switch off, but is kept thinking throughout the performance.

Influence of techniques on an audience

Some of Brecht's influence can be seen in techniques to make an audience take a step back and look at content in a different way. Here are some examples.

Set – minimal and not realistic, e.g. half curtain that doesn't hide a scene change or the actors changing costume. Use of placards and signs

Multimedia – projections of images and recorded film

Content and creative intention

Music – popular and appealing to everyone across society; performer sings in/out of role

Make-up, costume, masks, puppetry – exaggerated, representative and visual shortcuts to characterisation and attitude; different actors can take the same role; groups of people (police, workers) can all 'look' the same

Sound, lighting, special effects – the mechanics are made visible; live sound effects, visible microphones; it's a play, not reality

Now try this

Choose another practitioner. Consider how their style and techniques might influence your performance and communicate ideas to an audience.

You could think about how some performance material combines the styles of different practitioners, and how these might influence your work.

Influence of dance practitioners

Dance practitioners select and develop skills and techniques to communicate their intentions to an audience. They might be influenced by the skills and techniques used by other professional practitioners.

Selecting and developing skills and techniques

Consider the ways that choices of dance practitioners might influence your creative ideas. Here are three examples.

1 Inspiration

You might be inspired by, for example:

- the way a dance practitioner created the work to use movement styles to communicate their message
- the way they used production elements to enhance their meaning in performance.

2 Developing skills

The skills you develop might be influenced by the style of a practitioner who has trained to develop specific skills and techniques. For example:

- developing ballet technique, if influenced by Christopher Bruce
- participating in a Graham technique class to understand the technique Merce Cunningham rebelled against as part of the Martha Graham Dance Company
- taking part in workshops on ballet, tap, contemporary and jazz, to get closer to the style of Mia Michaels.

3 Realising creative intention

The creative intentions, interests and themes of practitioners may inspire your selection of skills and techniques. For example:

- Christopher Bruce and human rights: the harrowing images of death in *Ghost Dances* may inspire you to find new ways of showing death.
- Matthew Bourne and old Hollywood films such as those starring Fred Astaire: old Hollywood glamour may inspire music choices and the overall look of your piece.
- Lea Anderson and images: interesting artwork may inspire innovative body shapes and movements.

Skills and techniques used in *Ghost Dances* by Christopher Bruce include turnout, hip flexibility, good balance and teamwork.

Contact improvisation requires strength, weight placements and counterbalance. A pioneer was Steve Paxton, who also explored non-dance movement, e.g. walking, sitting and eating. You could include strength-building exercises into your warm ups and do an everyday movements activity.

Now try this

Choose a dance practitioner whose work you are familiar with. Identify how they use dance skills and techniques to communicate meaning. How might they influence your own work?

Influences on dance

Your own **skills and techniques** could be influenced by dance practitioners. For example, Bob Fosse is one of the most influential dance practitioners of the 20th century.

Bob Fosse

He choreographed many famous musicals such as *Cabaret*, *Sweet Charity* and *Chicago*. His style and choreography can inspire steps and movements, such as soft boiled egg hand shape, pigeon toed, splayed hands, crescent jump, use of hips and hunched shoulders.

Fosse technique uses the imagery of soft boiled eggs to help make the right shape with the hands for this movement. Movements such as these can be improved through practising hand shaping.

The position used in *Rich Man's Frug* requires a strong core and thigh muscles. Movements such as these can be improved through group warm-up exercises.

In this variation of the crescent jump, the torso and legs move to one side in the air, making a crescent shape in the body. Movements such as these need good elevation and extension that can be improved through technique classes. Developing your knee bend (plié) and use of the feet through ballet exercises will improve your elevation. Improving your general strength will also improve your extension.

Now try this

Watch some video footage of how Fosse uses hip isolations. Identify how you could develop these moves through exercises and activities, so that you can improve your own hip isolations and be able to perform the Fosse style of movement. Could this influence your choreography?

Influence of musical theatre practitioners

The creation of work and performance styles can be influenced by the ways that well-known musical theatre practitioners select and develop skills and techniques to communicate their creative intentions.

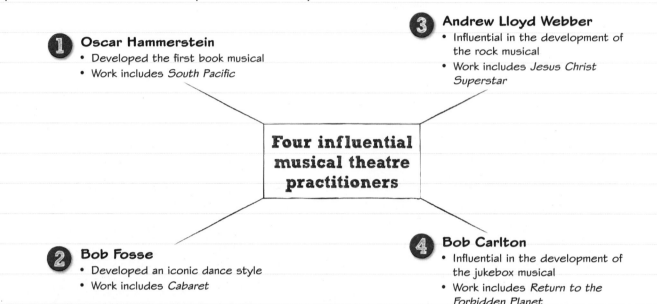

1 Oscar Hammerstein
- Developed the first book musical
- Work includes *South Pacific*

3 Andrew Lloyd Webber
- Influential in the development of the rock musical
- Work includes *Jesus Christ Superstar*

Four influential musical theatre practitioners

2 Bob Fosse
- Developed an iconic dance style
- Work includes *Cabaret*

4 Bob Carlton
- Influential in the development of the jukebox musical
- Work includes *Return to the Forbidden Planet*

Selecting and developing skills and techniques

When exploring skills and techniques used by practitioners, consider the different ways they might influence your creative ideas. Here are three examples, based on exploring a **book musical** and **Oscar Hammerstein**.

1 Acting skills

Show Boat is a book musical where songs and dance routines are fully integrated into the story. The style of acting employed in book musicals is usually naturalistic – sections of dialogue are used to move the plot along and portray the relationships between the characters.

2 Singing skills

Rodgers and Hammerstein created a light musical style that borrowed from jazz and popular music. Leading roles such as Laurie (*Oklahoma!*) and Maria (*The Sound of Music*) need well-trained voices. Supporting roles such as Will Parker (*Oklahoma!*) are less vocally demanding but require comedy and dance skills.

3 Dance skills

Narrative dance sequences can be used as well as dance routines. *Oklahoma!* has a 15-minute 'dream ballet' sequence. It was originally choreographed by Agnes de Mille and performed by dancers. In the 1998 National Theatre production, director Trevor Nunn broke with tradition, and the performers playing Laurie and Curly also performed the dance sequence.

Now try this

Choose a character from a book musical you have watched (e.g. Sandy in *Grease*, Seymour in *Little Shop of Horrors*, Nancy in *Oliver!*). Note what acting, singing and dance skills and techniques were used by the performer playing the role.

How might the skills and techniques you have identified influence your own creative ideas?

Influences on musical theatre

Musical theatre practitioners can influence the way **skills and techniques** are developed for creative intentions within different genres. For example, the jukebox musical emerged as a new genre of musical theatre in the late 20th century, and early practitioners influenced its development.

Bob Carlton – *Return to the Forbidden Planet*

Ben Elton – *We Will Rock You*

Some influential jukebox musical practitioners

Alan Janes – *Buddy – The Buddy Holly Story*

Catherine Johnson, Benny Andersson, Björn Ulvaeus – *Mamma Mia!*

Music performance skills

Early examples of the genre often required performers to play musical instruments as well as sing, act and dance.

- The role of Cookie in *Return to the Forbidden Planet* requires a performer who can play lead guitar to a high standard.
- *We Will Rock You*, a musical based around the songs of Queen, requires performers with 'rock' voices.

Acting, dance and specialist skills

While performers in jukebox musicals still need to be able to act, leading roles often don't require a high level of dance skills.

Consider any specialist skills you have, such as playing a musical instrument. How could these skills be integrated into your performance piece to help communicate your intentions to your audience?

Return to the Forbidden Planet

Return to the Forbidden Planet is one of the earliest examples of a jukebox musical, and won Best Musical at the 1990 Olivier Awards.

- ✓ It is based on a 1950s science-fiction film that was in turn based on Shakespeare's play *The Tempest*.
- ✓ The score uses a range of pop and rock standards from the 1950s and 1960s.
- ✓ An onstage band is used.
- ✓ It includes elements of audience participation.

Now try this

Consider a group of performers you work with to create a small group performance. Undertake a skills audit of the performers, listing acting, dance and singing skills, as well as any specialist skills. Which style/genre of musical theatre would suit the skills of the group?

How might the skills and techniques you have identified influence your own creative ideas?

Skills for young audiences

Young audiences fall into three broad categories: pre-school children, primary-aged children and teenagers.

Content for younger audiences

The **skills** required for performance pieces for a younger audience often link to suitable content.
Here are four examples.

1 **Familiar stories**

- Children like seeing characters they know. Theatre works based on films and popular children's stories are common.
- For example, the Unicorn Theatre's production of *Not Now, Bernard* is based on a picture book by David McKee, and is aimed at children over the age of three.

2 **Fairy tales**

- Children can often identify with fairy-tale characters and simple, easy-to-understand plots.
- For example, Matthew Bourne's *Cinderella* updates a traditional fairy tale and sets it in London during the Second World War. The show is aimed at all ages, including children from the age of five upwards.

3 **Animals**

- Pieces where some characters are animals, toys or fantasy creatures are popular with children. Where characters are given human or childlike qualities, children can easily understand their motivations and thoughts.
- For example, Polka Theatre's production of *Babe, the Sheep-Pig* includes a sheepdog and a herd of sheep as well as the title character, Babe the pig. It is recommended for ages five to eleven.

4 **Relevant issues**

- Theatre is a good medium for the exploration of issues affecting young people, relevant to the age group. The drama allows difficult issues to be explored in a safe environment.
- For example, Little Fish Theatre's production *Kiss and Tell* explores teenage sexual relationships and the law. It is aimed at teenagers aged 14–16.

Performance skills for younger audiences

Practitioners of children's theatre need to be versatile, as productions often require a range of skills.
Here are four examples.

1 **Acting**

- Acting styles are often heightened.
- Narration is common.
- Actors often 'break the fourth wall' to address the audience directly.
- Actors can lead audience participation and interactive elements.

2 **Dance**

- Pieces can be dance-based and use a range of performance styles, such as ballet, contemporary and urban.
- Dance can also be used to add interest to a drama-based piece.

3 **Singing and music**

- Song can be used to mark a point within the plot and/or create interest.
- Simple songs can be taught to the audience so that they can participate.
- Live accompaniment of songs is common.

4 **Design**

- Props can often be larger than life.
- Sets are often a flexible design as many companies tour to different types of venues.
- Costumes may need to be eye-catching.
- Puppets and masks are often used to portray animals and supernatural creatures.

Now try this

Consider a piece of performance work aimed at a young audience, and watch an extract if you can.

Note down the performance and design skills needed to communicate the features of the piece. How do they meet the needs of the target audience?

You could look at a website for a performance. Notice if it includes information on a recommended age for young audiences.

Skills for wide audiences

Performing arts practitioners often create work intended to appeal to a wide audience. This means skills must be selected and developed to engage people of various ages, different backgrounds and a range of interests.

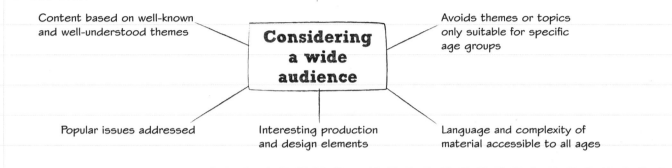

Content based on well-known and well-understood themes

Considering a wide audience

Avoids themes or topics only suitable for specific age groups

Popular issues addressed

Interesting production and design elements

Language and complexity of material accessible to all ages

Musical theatre

Musical theatre is one of the most popular forms of live theatre, with productions such as *The Lion King*, *Les Misérables* and *Wicked*. Different performance and design skills are required for a production such as *Wicked*, and successful musical theatre performers are often known as **triple threats**.

1 Singing skills

Musical theatre performers must have strong singing voices and the ability to learn songs quickly and accurately. For example, roles in musicals by Stephen Sondheim such as *Sweeney Todd* are challenging, as the music is difficult to perform. The role of Mrs Lovett in the original Broadway production was played by Angela Lansbury.

2 Acting skills

The ability to portray a character convincingly and deliver spoken dialogue is important. For example, the role of Mama Rose in *Gypsy* requires strong acting skills to portray an ambitious and bossy matriarch. Imelda Staunton played Rose in the 2015 West End revival of *Gypsy*.

3 Dance skills

A range of dance styles including jazz and tap are necessary. For example, the musical *Billy Elliot* needs a child performer with exceptional dance skills. Liam Mower played Billy and went on to perform with Matthew Bourne's company New Adventures. Their productions such as *Edward Scissorhands* and *Sleeping Beauty* reached a wide audience, telling the story entirely through music and dance skills.

Drama

Popular dramatic productions often have elements that stand out from more traditional productions. For example, *The Play that Goes Wrong* is a comedy based on the fictitious Cornley Polytechnic Drama Society. Disasters happen to the cast including forgetting lines, missing cues, broken props and items of set collapsing. Significant acting skills are required as movement must be perfectly choreographed to ensure physical jokes work, and lines must be carefully paced to allow for audience laughter.

Physical skills

Popular shows often require physical skills. For example, *The Curious Incident of the Dog in the Night-Time*, based on a book by Mark Haddon, uses multimedia elements to create the world as perceived by an autistic young man, Christopher. Physical performance skills are required as he is lifted to create the impression he is flying. Actors must also interact with the complex projected multimedia elements created for the show.

Now try this

Using the theme 'The Birthday Party', create some initial ideas for a performance piece that might appeal to a wide audience. Note the skills needed to successfully realise the piece.

Vocal skills

The chosen performance genre and style will inform decisions when selecting and developing vocal skills and techniques for performance.

Voice and performance

How voices are used in performance has an impact on the audience. Performers consider what they want the audience to understand about characters and events. Decisions are based on the performance style selected, and the role in performance. For example:

Performance style	Naturalistic (realism) or non-naturalistic (stylised)
Character/role	Age, gender, accent/dialect, social class, time period
Possible requirements of character/role	**Speaking:** quickly; lots of dialogue; snappy exchanges with other characters; directly to the audience; choral speaking
	Singing: solo; with others; accompanied by musicians
	Performance: highly physical

Character and expression

It is vital that the audience understands what a character wants. Your voice needs to **communicate the interpretation** of a character or role effectively. To demonstrate your character's objectives and context, make sure you know:

- what your character's objectives are – what they want in any scene or song
- what your character is doing – who they are talking to, where they are and why they are there.

This performer is using his voice to communicate expressively and engage the audience with what the character wants.

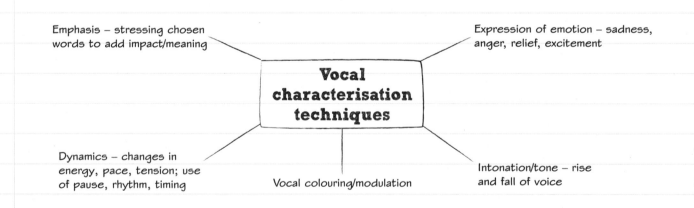

Emphasis – stressing chosen words to add impact/meaning

Expression of emotion – sadness, anger, relief, excitement

Vocal characterisation techniques

Dynamics – changes in energy, pace, tension; use of pause, rhythm, timing

Vocal colouring/modulation

Intonation/tone – rise and fall of voice

Now try this

You need to exercise your mouth and face to help ensure you speak or sing clearly. Find and note down:

- two breathing exercises
- one vocal projection exercise
- five tongue twisters.

Voice preparation

Performers prepare their voices for rehearsal and performance so they can communicate ideas clearly and effectively to an audience.

Vocal techniques

Vocal technique is necessary for an actor or singer to perform a role successfully. The audience must hear clearly and understand what is being spoken or sung. Here are three important ways.

1 **Breath control** on stage supports your voice and allows it to project without shouting or damaging your vocal chords. It can also help you avoid running out of breath during long speeches or songs.

2 **Voice projection** is about ensuring your voice fills the performance space, without straining your voice or shouting.

3 **Articulation** makes sure the words you say can be understood clearly, e.g. a particular combination of words, or speaking/singing at speed.

Posture

Use of **good posture** is an important vocal skill.

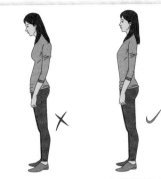

For good posture, keep your body relaxed and free from tension and feet shoulder width apart. Imagine a string running up through your body and out of the top of your head.

1 **Body warm-up**
- Stand centred
- Stretch your limbs
- Shake out tension from your body
- Massage your face and neck

Four warm-ups to prepare the voice

3 **Breathing exercises**
- Breathe out, making sounds such as hmmm, maaa, meee, may, ooo, ahhh

2 **Face warm-up**
- Massage your jaw
- Pretend to chew toffee
- Blow raspberries

4 **Vocal warm-up**
- Count to eight on the musical scale
- Sing a song/recite lines
- Say tongue twisters

This performer is doing a face warm-up. Face warm-ups also include massaging your jaw. This improves your resonance and helps you to project your voice. You can use your hands to check that your face is resonating (vibrating).

Now try this

Research and prepare a five-minute vocal warm-up for a group rehearsal.

You could add a specific vocal warm-up with a selected song or dialogue, to experiment with different emotions.

Physical performance skills

The selection of individual physical skills depends on:

- the performance discipline – e.g. dance, musical theatre, acting
- the performance style – e.g. street dance, rock opera, influences such as Brecht.

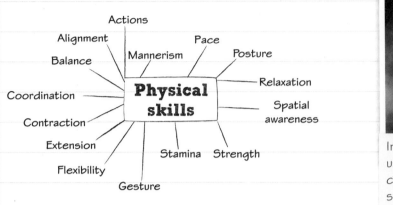

Physical skills: Actions, Alignment, Mannerism, Pace, Balance, Posture, Coordination, Relaxation, Contraction, Spatial awareness, Extension, Stamina, Strength, Flexibility, Gesture

In this contemporary dance, the performers use physical skills including balance, flexibility, coordination, spatial awareness, strength and stamina to create an artistic performance.

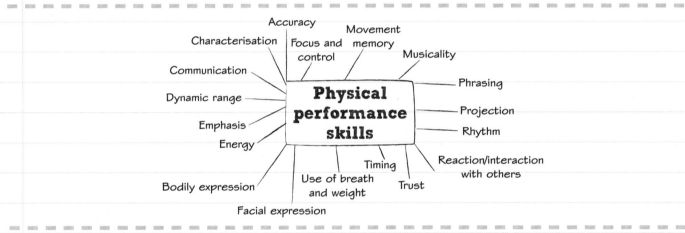

Physical performance skills: Accuracy, Characterisation, Focus and control, Movement memory, Musicality, Communication, Phrasing, Dynamic range, Projection, Emphasis, Rhythm, Energy, Reaction/interaction with others, Bodily expression, Use of breath and weight, Timing, Trust, Facial expression

Selecting skills

Creative decisions about a performance will inform what physical skills to select and develop.

- Physical theatre or dance performance require stamina.
- Naturalistic acting performance requires reaction/interaction with others.
- Specialist dances in specific styles require dedicated physical skills, e.g. jazz dance.

Warm-ups and cool-downs

Warm-ups should include pulse-raising exercises as well as movements to mobilise and stretch the muscles. **Cool-downs** should include slower exercises which bring the heart rate back down to its usual pace. They can also include relaxation techniques and stretches.

Developing skills

Physical skills are developed in rehearsals through warm-ups and workshops. Design these to be specific to your individual performance needs. For example:

- **for improving stamina**: include some extended aerobic activity within the warm-up
- **for improving reaction/interaction with others**: include games and activities such as zip zap boing
- **for improving flexibility**: stretch
- **for improving focus**: include focus walks or focus on specific skills – e.g. singing a love song to a partner who must remain straight-faced could help if the comedy in the scene is distracting.

Review your performance regularly to find the skills you need to improve.

Now try this

Conduct an audit of your physical skills. Identify three areas to improve and how you could improve them.

Use the lists above to help with your audit.

Acting performance skills

Practitioners refine physical, vocal and interpretive performance skills so they can fully communicate with an audience.

Reflecting on skills

Acting performance skills can be improved through self-reflection and analysis, such as:

- feedback on performance techniques
- recording rehearsals and watching them back for an objective record of skills and what needs to be improved.

To improve performance skills, you must know what they are and how to apply them. Here are examples of **three** groups of skills.

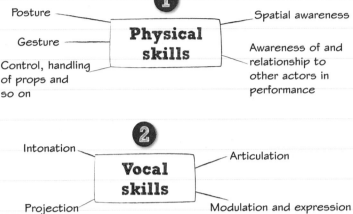

1 Physical skills
- Posture
- Gesture
- Control, handling of props and so on
- Spatial awareness
- Awareness of and relationship to other actors in performance

2 Vocal skills
- Intonation
- Projection
- Articulation
- Modulation and expression

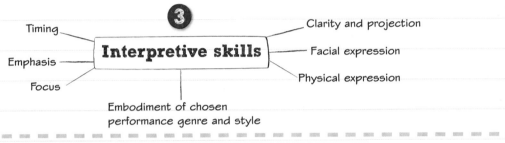

3 Interpretive skills
- Timing
- Emphasis
- Focus
- Embodiment of chosen performance genre and style
- Clarity and projection
- Facial expression
- Physical expression

Developing acting skills

An action plan can be used to develop identified performance skills and build them into individual and group rehearsals. Here is an example.

In my acting piece I ...	What is the problem?	Why?	Action plan
... have to catch objects thrown at me.	I keep missing the objects.	Poor hand-eye coordination.	Practise throwing a ball against a wall and catching it.
... do a physical piece that requires moving and speaking continuously.	I'm out of breath towards the end.	Poor stamina.	Jogging, cross-training, swimming.
... need to perform a realistic portrayal of an old man.	I don't look or sound like an old man.	Lack of confidence in acting.	Character development workshops.
... need to do a regional accent.	I can't get it right and jump from accent to accent.	Not enough practice.	Listen to others speaking in the accent and copy them.
... have to say a long sequence of numbers as part of the script.	I can't remember the sequence.	Poor concentration.	Break down and repeat the sequence.

Now try this

Think about a performance where you or your group struggled with some performance skills. Use an action plan like the one above to show how those skills could be improved.

See also the physical skills revised on page 32.

Dance performance skills

The selection and development of dance performance skills allows the group to communicate creative intentions to an audience.

Selecting skills

Creative decisions about a performance will inform the dance skills and techniques the group selects and develops. Consider the ideas of the group and what is needed for the choreography and movement.

Reflecting on skills

The dance performance skills of the group can be identified through reflection and analysis, to ensure a strong performance. Developing those skills is an ongoing commitment.

reflect on the skills of the group → practise → perform → evaluate → set actions for improvement → (cycle)

Using mirrors and video

Using mirrors is a good way to help you self-evaluate. However, video recording group rehearsals and watching them back will allow you to give your all during a run-through, and clearly see what needs to be worked on.

Recording group rehearsals allows you to evaluate and develop the performance skills of the group.

Developing dance skills

An action plan can be used to develop identified dance performance skills and build them into individual and group rehearsals. Here is an example.

In my dance I ...	What is the problem?	Why?	Action plan
... go from the floor to standing quickly.	I have to put my hand down.	Weak back and core muscles.	Sit-ups, back-lifts, T-raisers.
... dance for 10 minutes at high impact.	I'm out of breath and shabby at the end.	Poor stamina.	Jogging, cross-training, swimming.
... have the character of an old lady.	I feel and look silly so I'm not good at it.	Lack of confidence in acting.	Workshops to develop character.
... drop to the splits.	I can't do it.	Inflexible.	Stretches.
... use a difficult canon sequence.	I end up in time with another dancer.	Not counting the movement right.	Break down and repeat the sequence.

Now try this

Think about the last dance move you or your group struggled to perform. Use an action plan like the one above to show how those skills could be improved.

Musical theatre performance skills

Skill selection in musical theatre will depend on the style of the work and its creative intentions. With singing skills you will need to consider song styles, individual and group strengths, and interpretive singing skills.

Song styles and singing skills

The style of the music will inform the singing skills and techniques to be used. A song in a rock music style will require a different style of singing to a light classical piece, for example.

Consider ideas for appropriate songs and whether these fit with the style of your piece and the skills of the performers in your group.

Reflecting on skills

To develop musical skills you must identify, apply and improve them through reflection on, for example:

- **intonation** – singing in tune with accurate pitch
- **projection** – controlling the volume of the voice using the body's resonators
- **articulation** – pronunciation of sounds, particularly consonants
- **tonal quality** – the character of the voice, e.g. clear or breathy.

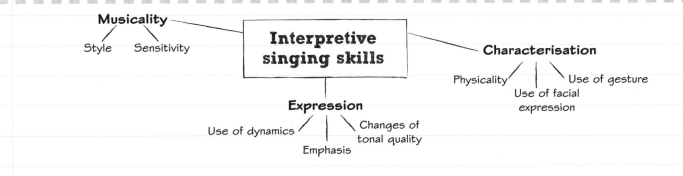

Developing singing skills

An action plan can be used to develop singing skills and build them into individual and group rehearsals. Here is an example.

In the song I ...	What is the problem?	Why?	Action plan
... lack confidence in the verse sections.	I am unsure of the tune and the lyrics.	I need to be more familiar with it.	Save the song onto my phone and listen to it until I know it.
... find the end section with higher notes difficult.	My voice sounds strained and breaking.	It takes time for my voice to warm up to reach higher notes.	Warm up properly before I sing.
... stumble over the lyrics at the end of the chorus.	This section is fast and I can't get my tongue round the words.	I need to improve my articulation.	Practise the section slowly then gradually build up the speed.
... find it difficult to maintain the characterisation.	I am not communicating my character's intentions in the song.	I don't understand some of the lyrics.	Go over the lyrics as if it was a monologue, and work to understand my character better.
... struggle with the key change at the end of the song.	I keep going off key.	I can't find the right note to come in on.	Save the song to my phone and listen to the key change until it is really familiar.

Now try this

In relation to singing skills, identify your main strengths and areas for development. Use an action plan like the one above to show how you can achieve your targets.

Acting group improvisation

Improvisation is a spontaneous and excellent way of selecting and developing group performance skills and techniques to realise creative ideas. Here are **four** approaches.

❶ Physical

Decisions about a character's physicality can be made through improvisation, e.g. exploring the movements of young children or older people.

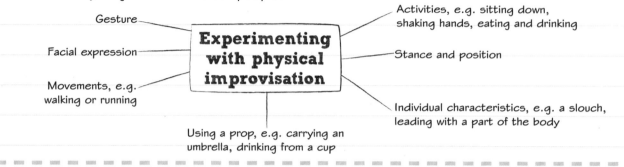

❷ Aural

Decisions about a character's voice and characteristics could be made through improvisation, such as speaking, singing, using the body as a percussive instrument (e.g. slapping and tapping) or wider exploration into sound effects.

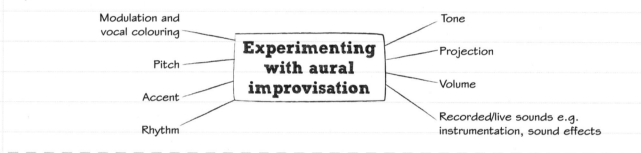

❸ Techniques and methods

Improvisation can be informed by influential practitioners.

- Mike Leigh, theatre and film director, asks actors to develop a character based on people they know, creating detail from factors such as parents, background, upbringing and education. The improvisations are recorded and the best parts are scripted, forming a story outline.
- Keith Johnstone specialises in theatre improvisation. He developed a set of rules where, for example, if someone in role suggests a situation you are in, you do not block it but incorporate it in your next spoken line or physical reaction.

❹ Practical exploration

When practically exploring through improvisation as an actor, try the following tasks:

- Focus on the stimulus.
- Use your imagination to think 'outside the box'.
- Maintain physical and vocal identity if improvising in character.
- Using an existing play or production as your inspiration, improvise a new scene using the existing style or a different one.
- Film your improvisation to generate material for your performance.

Now try this

1 Choose a theme, situation and performance style.
2 Perform a movement/vocal improvisation for one minute only. If possible, record the improvisation and watch it back.
3 Consider how it could generate ideas to form the basis of a scene.

Consider:
- where you are
- who you are
- what you want.

Dance group improvisation

Dance improvisation can be used as a group to develop skills and techniques to realise creative intentions. Practitioners can set rules so they explore with purpose, and the restrictions can help to make the process creative and effective. Here are **four** approaches.

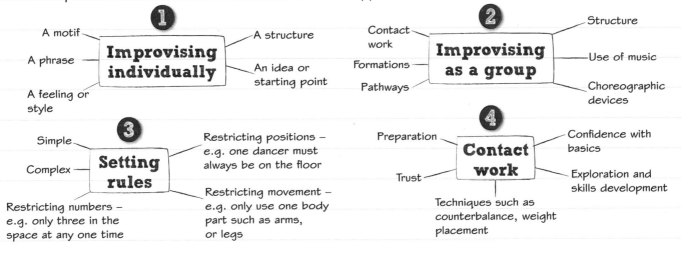

Building confidence and trust

It is important to prepare for group improvisation by building confidence and trust. Here are some examples.

Activity	Building confidence and trust
Focus walks	Identify three points in space and walk towards each one.
Count to 20	As a group, take it in turns as you count up to 20. No hesitations. No more than one person speaks at the same time.
Group stops and starts	Walk around the room and come to a collective stop. Then start again. No leaders. Think as a unit.
Trust falls	Fall into a partner's arms. Start small with a lean, and build up.
Trust circles	Stand in a circle around one person. The person in the middle leans and is supported by the hands of the group, first with eyes open then with eyes closed.
Leading a partner	Walk around the room with a partner who has their eyes closed. Steer them carefully by their shoulders, so that they don't bump into anyone else. Then swap over.

Developing skills

- ✓ You can use improvisation skills to develop other performance skills. For example, by improvising to different music, you could enhance your musicality.
- ✓ You could also improve your live performance skills. Going wrong or forgetting a move in live performance can be daunting. A true professional will think on their feet and improvise back into the routine.
- ✓ Recording improvisations can help you review what works well.

Now try this

Using the ideas on this page, set some rules for a group dance improvisation.

Using instrumental music to improvise to gives you more freedom of expression.

Musical theatre group improvisation

Group improvisation skills can be used to develop musical theatre. For example, practitioners can develop musical elements of a piece to explore chosen material and develop new ways of presenting it. Here are **three** approaches.

① Improvising a harmony vocal line

Harmonising is when you sing above or below the tune to create harmony, using notes that complement those of the melody.

To develop improvising, try the following tasks:

- Start with a song that has a simple structure and uses a small number of chords.
- Don't try to harmonise until you know the tune very well.
- Go slowly to begin with, for example by humming long notes that only change when the chords of the song do.
- Mirror the shape of the melody. If the melody goes up, so should the harmony.
- Include notes that are a third or sixth apart, as these usually sound good together. For example, if the melody note is C, then E or A will work as a harmony note.
- Record your work on a mobile device so that you don't lose something that works well.

② Call and response backing vocals

Adding backing vocals is a good way to improvise and develop a song. A common form of backing vocal uses call and response. This is where main vocalist sings a line which is 'answered' by the backing vocalists.

The answer might be:

- a repetition of the original line (like an echo)
- a repetition of part of the original line
- an answer to the original line.

③ Characterisation and physicality

Decisions about a character's physicality during the delivery of a song can be made through improvisation. Treat the song as if it were a monologue. Consider the character's intentions, and improvise movement and gesture to enhance their communication.

Communication of a character's intentions can be informed by improvisation of gesture and movement during rehearsal, creating a powerful performance, as in *Ghost the Musical*.

Now try this

Choose a song from musical theatre that is familiar or that inspires you. Identify some ideas that could be developed through improvisation, and note how you might do this.

Developing acting style and genre

To develop style and genre to communicate creative intentions, performers and designers need to know the rules and make performance decisions. For example:

- **comedy:** funny or silly
- **tragedy:** serious in terms of subject matter and tone
- **docudrama:** focuses on real people and events
- **physical theatre:** uses physicality
- **naturalism:** everyday movement and speech
- **Epic:** exaggerated gesture, facial expression and movement
- **farce:** elements of slapstick and comic timing
- **mime:** physical expression with an absence of spoken language.

Using stylistic features to develop the piece

When developing style and genre, identify the key features and how they inform your performance. Here are some examples.

Genre/style	A key feature	Example of how it can inform performance
Comedy – naturalism	Comic timing	Deliver a line, a facial expression or a gesture to have comic impact
Tragedy – social drama	Believable emotional response	Show that your character is visibly upset
Physical theatre – mime	Interaction with imaginary objects	Move through an abandoned factory

Developing skills to perform the styles

To perform in a particular style, you need to develop particular skills. For example, if miming a character moving through an environment, mime skills need to indicate where you are (what surrounds you), what you encounter (e.g. showing the weight of an object), and how your character reacts (e.g. your focus and physical performance). You can focus on **three** key performance elements:

1 Facial expression

- Perform exercises to clearly indicate emotion and response to situation, or physical reaction to impact of imaginary objects.

- Practise emotional responses in the mirror. Exaggerate facial expressions to show emotional response to a situation, such as squeezing your body through a tight space, grabbing something hot, or wading through very cold water.

2 Body positioning and movement

- Perform exercises to strengthen your core to help demonstrate the weight and physical energy of objects.

- Practise with real objects to learn their weight, shape and size. Which parts of your body are used during an action? For example, if carrying a heavy box, is the weight distributed in your thighs? How are your arms positioned to carry the box? Does your face show the pain of the weight? Now try to mime carrying a heavy box and try to capture the same physical positioning and focus.

3 Vocal expression

- Perform exercises to develop vocal expression, including how to show an emotional response to a situation.

- Practise a vocal response to the situation but avoid using words, e.g. tut, grunt, groan, scream, whimper. Use different ways to express discomfort or pain.

Now try this

Select a performance you have enjoyed. Note down how performers and designers use their skills to realise the style and genre when communicating their ideas to the audience.

Developing dance style and genre

Performers and designers develop the chosen styles and genre of the dance piece to communicate their ideas to the audience.

Knowing the rules

It is important to know the rules of the chosen styles and genre. You can then consider the ways you wish to keep or break them. Here are four key questions.

1 Are there specific movements you must use?

2 What are the most evident dynamic qualities?

3 What kind of music is the dance normally performed with?

4 Is there a specific way the movement is structured or choreographed?

Keeping informed

Do you need to know more about the styles? You could:

☑ take technique classes

☑ watch professional pieces

☑ read articles or interviews

☑ watch documentaries on the style.

Using stylistic features to develop the piece

When developing styles and genre, identify the key features and how they inform your piece. Here are some examples.

Genre/style	A key feature	Example of how it can inform your piece
Jazz – Fosse	Hunched shoulders	Changing normal walks to ones with hunched shoulders during transitions
Street dance – waacking	Fast arm movements	Speeding up the arm movements and gestures to quicken the pace and rhythm
Contemporary – Graham	Contraction	Showing emotional pain through contractions

Developing skills to perform the styles

To develop genre and style you also need to develop the required skills. For example, if you are using waacking in your piece and have choreographed a section that is fast-paced in keeping with the style, you will need strong arms as well as a good range of mobility. You could improve:

- **arm strength** using exercises to increase strength in the upper body such as press-ups, weights or tricep-dips
- **mobility** by circling the arms and shoulders, and using wall and tricep stretches.

You can embed stylistic qualities into your warm up and technical exercises so that you practise the style in each session.

Now try this

Consider a dance performance you have enjoyed. Note down how performers and designers use their skills to realise the style and genre when communicating their ideas to the audience.

Developing musical theatre style and genre

Decisions that performers and designers make about style and genre will provide a framework for developing the work and the performance skills needed to fully realise the work.

Music/singing
- Pop
- Rock
- Light classical/lyrical

Analysing the style

Acting
- Comedy
- Physical theatre
- Puppetry
- Naturalistic
- Non-naturalistic

Dance
- Jazz
- Contemporary
- Ballet
- Tap
- Commercial

Using stylistic features to develop the piece

When developing style and genre, identify the key features and how they inform your performance. Here are some examples.

Genre/style	Key features	Ways of working
Rock musical	Rock vocals and backing vocals	Develop backing vocals through improvisation
	Commercial dance styles	Watch commercial dance videos for inspiration for choreography
Mid-20th century book musical	Light classical singing	Work on characterisation in songs
	Naturalistic acting	Undertake some naturalistic acting exercises e.g. the 'magic if'

Developing skills to perform the styles

To perform in a particular style, you need to develop the skills to do so. For example, if you are performing a song in a light classical style, you will need to work on the placement of your voice in order to create the clear tone associated with this style.

Legit

'Legit' is a term often used for a genre of musical theatre singing. It is used where the singing is rooted in classical, traditional voice training, vocal style and technique. The term is short for 'legitimate'. It does not mean that other musical theatre vocal genres and styles are inferior or 'illegitimate'.

Taking singing classes to work on specific vocal exercises will improve your voice placement.

Now try this

Select a musical theatre performance you have enjoyed. Note down how performers and designers use their skills to realise the style and genre when communicating their ideas to the audience.

Individual preparation

Performers and designers need to develop individual skills, techniques and personal management skills to take part in the rehearsal process.

Learning and absorbing material

Preparing for rehearsal may involve memorising lines, movements and songs.

Repetition: perform small sections many times. Memorise line by line. Practise with someone reading your cue lines

Writing: make notes or write reminders

Drawing images: connect visual moments to learn choreography, movements, blocking and stage directions

Techniques used for learning and memorising

Video recording: watch yourself perform to help experiment with interpretation, development of character and ways to communicate themes and ideas

Audio recording: listen to yourself reading/singing through headphones. You could record other characters' lines and leave a gap for your lines

Think about it: when you get a spare moment, think through the action and what you are supposed to do, as if you are watching yourself do it

Developing individual skills

In preparation for rehearsal, you will need to practise so that you achieve your best contribution to performance.

- List the **skills** and **techniques** that are most significant for your role, and practise them regularly. For example, you could focus on projection, musicality, facial expression or contrast.

- List the **creative intentions** in relation to the brief and stimulus, and map them to your individual contribution. Practise **communicating** those intentions.

- Take part in movement or **technique classes** to develop your skills outside rehearsals. If your performance is in a jazz dance style, take part in jazz technique classes. Movement classes will also help with general fitness.

- Rehearse and perform for family or friends. Ask for **feedback** on what you could do better.

Personal management skills

Taking part in the rehearsal process requires a high level of individual commitment and preparation. Consider these **four** important ways.

 Attendance: always attend rehearsals. Absence slows the creative and rehearsal processes, and affects the quality of performance.

 Attire: dress appropriately for a safe and professional rehearsal and performance.

 Punctuality: always be on time and take part in warm-ups and discussion. This will strengthen your performance.

Deadlines: make careful plans and meet deadlines so that the creative process is strong in rehearsal and you achieve the best quality of performance and design.

Skills log

When keeping a skills log, note your skills development and contribution to group preparation as part of the rehearsal process. For example, demonstrate how you:

- ✓ set yourself goals
- ✓ prioritise tasks
- ✓ make lists and schedules
- ✓ spread out your tasks
- ✓ avoid procrastination
- ✓ stay level-headed
- ✓ keep proactive
- ✓ stay organised
- ✓ keep self-motivated.

See pages 54–69 to revise what is needed for your skills log.

Now try this

List three skills and/or techniques that you know could be improved. Identify an exercise you could do each day to improve these skills/techniques.

 This could be a drama game, a vocal exercise, a physical exercise, or a design development.

Group rehearsals

Group rehearsal skills are an essential part of the rehearsal and performance process. Performers and designers use them to realise creative ideas in response to a brief.

Managing rehearsal time

It is vital to plan how much time is needed to rehearse as a group, so the piece is ready by the performance date. Draw up a **rehearsal schedule** that includes milestones and deadlines, e.g.:

1 the first full run of a piece

2 the 'dress' rehearsal

3 the final performance.

Working as a group

To create an enjoyable and productive environment:

- be committed, punctual and appropriately dressed, warming up and cooling down
- be open-minded, respecting others' opinions and trying out everyone's ideas
- communicate effectively so you are clear on individual roles and responsibilities
- make notes on feedback and make necessary changes
- give and take instruction and direction by being clear, concise and listening to each other
- remain focused.

Contributing ideas

Part of the rehearsal process is continuing to share ideas. Listen carefully and build trust and cooperation with group members. Be constructive. This encourages creativity and enthusiasm, so you feel comfortable as you rehearse and perform side by side.

Not constructive	Constructive
👎 Your idea is no good.	👍 That idea might not work because …
👎 I don't like the last scene of the piece.	👍 I think the last scene could be improved if we …
👎 I am getting sick of your negative attitude.	👍 You seem really down. Can you tell me why?
👎 You still haven't learned your part.	👍 How can we help you learn your lines?

Progressing and refining skills

As you rehearse, consider how you will:

- **develop** performance or design skills according to your discipline
- **try out** exploratory techniques
- **share ideas** for structure, style, form and content
- **select** the best ideas and discard less relevant ones
- **extend**, **shape** and **refine** ideas
- **assess** and **improve** skills through repetition of material, using mirrors, recording or watching each other and providing feedback

- **create** a **practical** and **safe** performance space, learning blocking and stage directions
- **learn** dialogue, songs, movement and choreography
- **interpret** and develop a character
- **check progress** in relation to the brief, what your performance is about and its main intention(s)
- **identify** any problems and actively find positive solutions.

Now try this

1 Consider your own strengths and areas for development in relation to group rehearsal work. List any problems you encounter when developing your performance or design skills. What can you do to solve them?

2 Create an outline production schedule for a workshop performance.

Keep notes of your skills development. This will be useful for your skills log.

See pages 54–69 to revise what is needed for your skills log.

Performance skills and techniques

Performers demonstrate effective use of vocal, physical and interpretative skills and techniques in performance. These skills are used to communicate to an audience ideas of time and place, character and emotion.

Realising creative ideas

To realise creative ideas in performance, performers should be secure about decisions made in relation to content, genre, style, form and structure. This provides a solid platform for the effective use of performance skills and techniques.

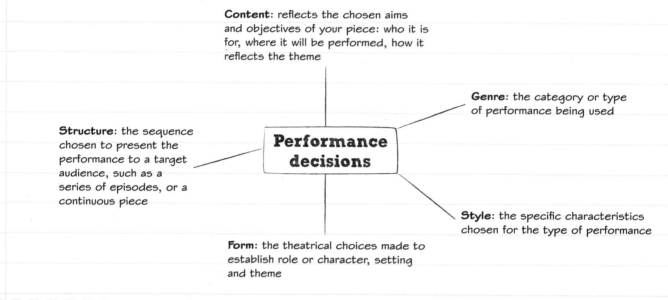

Content: reflects the chosen aims and objectives of your piece: who it is for, where it will be performed, how it reflects the theme

Genre: the category or type of performance being used

Structure: the sequence chosen to present the performance to a target audience, such as a series of episodes, or a continuous piece

Performance decisions

Style: the specific characteristics chosen for the type of performance

Form: the theatrical choices made to establish role or character, setting and theme

Developing performance skills

With the overall structure and content defined, here are **three** ways to ensure your performance skills communicate the work successfully to your audience, with the different techniques listed for each method.

1 Communication
- Genre/style/form
- Intention
- Interpretation
- Mood, tension
- Emotion
- Expression
- Language/accent
- With other performers
- With the audience

2 Performance
- Focus, control
- Vocalisation
- Physicality
- Projection
- Phrasing, emphasis
- Breathing, timing
- Stillness, gesture
- Dynamics, contrasts
- Characterisation

3 Material
- Cues and lines
- Music and songs
- Movements
- Performance space
- Settings: time, place
- Entrances and exits
- Levels, stage furniture
- Props
- Sound effects

Now try this

Choose one example from each of the three areas of performance skills and techniques above. Give a specific example of when you have used them in performance. Note down why they were successful or how they could be improved.

Consider how the impact on the audience helped communicate your intentions.

Sustaining performance

Performers need to be physically and mentally prepared to sustain the communication of ideas in performance. Here are **six** ways.

1 Be focused

Every performance requires:

- energy
- focus
- concentration
- commitment.

2 Be prepared

Performers develop stamina so they are:

- physically prepared, through strengthening exercises
- mentally prepared, knowing the performance material inside out
- in the moment, focusing on the task at hand.

3 Be adaptable

Even the best-planned work can be different in live performance. Performers:

- stay alert and in the moment, ready to adapt if someone misses a line, cue or movement
- sustain concentration and don't come out of character, pull a face, giggle or groan
- maintain the performance for the audience, so they don't notice if something goes wrong.

4 Be confident

Confidence is important in performance. Performers:

- memorise the performance material so they are not worried about forgetting it
- use techniques such as breathing, relaxation and mindfulness meditations to keep calm
- use their energy to inhabit their role with confidence.

5 Be impressive

There are key performance elements that most performers find hard to demonstrate:

- fluency
- control
- consistency
- attack
- charisma
- energy
- embodiment of character/role.

These can be achieved through a positive, hard-working attitude, and will impress an audience if practised enough.

6 Enjoy the performance

The most important thing when it comes to a good performance is a sense of enjoyment. Performers who invest time and effort into the development of work enjoy sharing it with others. Watching professional performers can help you understand their technique and attitude. Notice how they communicate with their audience. You could incorporate some of their techniques into your own performance.

Now try this

Prepare a ten-minute warm-up exercise that you could complete before taking part in a workshop performance.

You could prepare a physical warm-up and a vocal warm-up.

45

Preparing with others

It is important to communicate effectively with others when taking part in final preparations, which may include setting up/get-in and get-out/strike. The flowchart shows what a lead-up to a performance might include, where appropriate.

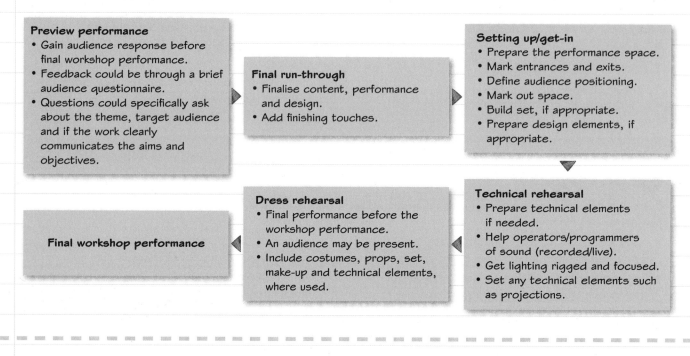

Preview performance
- Gain audience response before final workshop performance.
- Feedback could be through a brief audience questionnaire.
- Questions could specifically ask about the theme, target audience and if the work clearly communicates the aims and objectives.

Final run-through
- Finalise content, performance and design.
- Add finishing touches.

Setting up/get-in
- Prepare the performance space.
- Mark entrances and exits.
- Define audience positioning.
- Mark out space.
- Build set, if appropriate.
- Prepare design elements, if appropriate.

Technical rehearsal
- Prepare technical elements if needed.
- Help operators/programmers of sound (recorded/live).
- Get lighting rigged and focused.
- Set any technical elements such as projections.

Dress rehearsal
- Final performance before the workshop performance.
- An audience may be present.
- Include costumes, props, set, make-up and technical elements, where used.

Final workshop performance

Checklist for performance

☑ Make sure you have rehearsed effectively together.

☑ Be sure each member of the group is clear about individual roles and responsibilities.

☑ Memorise your material so that you know it off by heart, especially the first cue/line/entrance/song.

☑ Think about possible things that could go wrong, and find solutions.

☑ Check that design elements and resources are still relevant when rehearsing for performance. Make changes if required. Think about the basic requirements, and don't make designs too complex. Existing resources could be adapted.

☑ Make sure you have everything you need, e.g. props, and that everything is in place.

☑ Ensure any technical support is ready (if using music and so on).

☑ Make sure you have considered health and safety issues (e.g. no gum, socks or jewellery).

☑ Take part in individual and group warm-up and focus exercises.

☑ Think about the ways you communicate with each other and the audience.

☑ Be prepared for get-out/strike following the performance.

Now try this

Think about a specific performance you have been involved in. Prepare a checklist for final preparations that would ensure the group is communicating well and is fully prepared.

Performing with others

The best professional performers are in full control of their performance. The audience can relax and put their trust in confident performers.

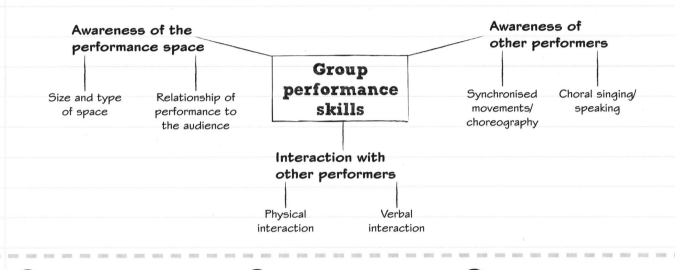

Awareness of the performance space
- Size and type of space
- Relationship of performance to the audience

Group performance skills

Interaction with other performers
- Physical interaction
- Verbal interaction

Awareness of other performers
- Synchronised movements/ choreography
- Choral singing/ speaking

① Performance space

The nature of the performance space impacts on the way a group performs together. For example, a smaller studio space:

- can be more intimate than a larger theatre
- can place the performer close to the audience
- can be flexible for where the audience sits.

② Other performers

Performers are aware of their own movements and those of others. For example, in dance and physical work:

- movement might be sequenced or synchronised
- meticulous rehearsal is required if moving in unison
- contact work requires careful planning.

③ Material

Physical and vocal work is often in response to other performers. For example:

- in a dualogue, each performer fully invests in listening and reacting to the work of their partner
- in musical theatre, an ensemble song requires listening and singing skills so that voices blend and no one overpowers.

Performing together

An action plan can be used for confidence in performance. Here is an example.

Problem	Example	Impact	Avoiding the problem
Forgetting dialogue	You forget your line and others improvise to cover it.	Lost rhythm and timing.	Know the whole script (e.g. learn all dialogue). Practise every day.
Forgetting next position/cue	You miss your entrance cue and have to catch up in performance.	Out of sync with music.	Refine each scene and sequence. Practise, evaluate, perform.
Unsure about character/role	You are playing two different characters but the audience can't tell them apart.	Lack of projection and clarity.	Develop the role. Practise, evaluate, interpret, practise.

Now try this

Watch an extract of theatre (drama, dance or musical theatre) that includes ensemble performance work. Consider the skills used by performers when they interact with each other.

Communicating ideas

Performers and designers use different ways to communicate ideas and intentions to an audience in a live performance.

Ideas and intentions

A performance needs to show the meaning of a piece in a way that relates to any brief and targets the audience. These three questions can help you assess how far you are communicating your ideas and intentions.

1 How have you used genre, structure and style?

2 Are your interpretation and performance and design skills well-chosen and clear?

3 How well do your choices meet the brief?

Targeting audience

These three questions can help you assess how well you are targeting your audience.

1 How far are your intentions and messages clear to your target audience?

2 Which parts could be clearer?

3 How can you improve?

Communication skills

Communication in performance takes place in a variety of ways, such as facial expression or tone of voice. Make sure your decisions are relevant to the overall performance and that you can explain and justify them.

This performer is communicating to the audience that they are an old character.

You can use physicality to demonstrate your character's age. Older pensioners rarely do high kicks and jump into the splits. Slower and limited movement would help in showing the audience you are an older character.

Improving communication of ideas

To successfully communicate with an audience, performers ensure they are always in role, focused and have clarity of movement throughout the performance. Here is a way to improve.

1 Do a run-through of your work to someone watching who can shout 'freeze' at any time, or identify a moment in your piece and stand in freeze-frame or tableau.

2 Each performer thinks about how they could improve their positioning, shape, focus and attitude at that instant.

3 Evaluate whether you are using your whole body and face to communicate meaning, and what you might change.

Now try this

Watch 'Tonight (Ensemble)' from *West Side Story*. Identify what each group/role is trying to communicate and how they are communicating it: Jets, Sharks, Anita, Tony, Maria and Riff. You can approach this from your own discipline, e.g. acting, musical theatre or dance.

Remember that performers consider:
- target audience and purpose (see also pages 3–4)
- developing skills that express and communicate creative intentions (see also page 20)
- skills needed for chosen audiences (see also pages 28–29).

Reflecting on process

After a performance, it is important to reflect on the working **process** leading up to it. Performers and designers do a lot of work to produce a live performance from a stimulus and idea. Think about what happened and how you shaped your work.

Response to the brief

Performers and designers consider how well they have responded to a brief by looking at notes taken during the process, and any recorded clips. Here are some questions to help with reflection.

- How did I generate ideas in response to the brief?
- Who was the target audience, and why was the audience selected?
- Was my intention clear?
- What structure/genre/style was used, and why?
- What resources were needed?
- How did props or the performance space enhance the piece?
- Are there parts that could have been clearer?
- How could I have achieved this?

Use of skills and techniques

Performers and designers reflect on how well they selected and used skills and techniques to generate and prepare material for performance. Here are some questions to help with reflection.

- What skills and techniques did I use? (physical, vocal, musical, design, interpretive)
- How far were they successful?
- Did I find some techniques more effective than others?
- How did the work of others influence the development of my skills and techniques?
- What did I do to improve my skills and techniques in time for performance?
- How did I rehearse?
- How did I record/document my selection and development of skills and techniques?
- What skills and techniques would I like to develop further?

Development and contribution of ideas

Performers and designers reflect on how ideas have developed during the process. Here are some questions to help with reflection.

- What ideas did I contribute?
- How far were they successful?
- Did I find it easy/difficult to communicate my ideas to my group?
- If I repeated the process, would I make any changes to my contribution?
- What were the contributions of others?

The process of shaping a performance includes developing ideas, skills and techniques in response to the brief. This involves decision-making, negotiation, pushing creative boundaries and commitment.

Now try this

Think back to the rehearsal process for your last live performance. Make notes on how effective you were during the rehearsal process. Could you have been better? If so, how?

⇐ Use clear bullet points.

Reflecting on the outcome

After a performance, it is important to evaluate audience feedback and reflect on key areas of your contribution to the live workshop **performance**.

Ways of evaluating

In a professional workshop performance, the performers and designers ask the audience for feedback and make changes in light of their comments. Here are some methods used to consider changes and ways of developing a performance further:

- post-performance question and answer session with the audience
- providing a questionnaire that the audience could complete, with or without giving their names
- speaking with the audience after the performance
- reviewing notes taken by performers and designers after the performance about what went well and what might be improved
- analysing any recordings of rehearsals and performance.

Communication

Performers and designers consider how well they **communicated ideas** through their role, and communicated with **other** performers and designers. Here are some questions to help with reflection.

- How far was my intention clear?
- Were there parts that could have been clearer?
- How could they have been made clearer?
- What was the impact of the structure/style/genre in performance?
- If I were to revisit this performance, what would I do differently?

Application of skills

Performers and designers reflect on how well they used **skills** and **techniques** when contributing to a workshop performance. Here are some questions to help with reflection.

- What was the impact of my performance or design skills and techniques?
- Did some performance or design skills and techniques have more impact than others? Why?
- Which skills and techniques would I develop for future performances?
- How would they enhance the performance?

Overall impact of performance

When considering the overall impact of the performance, the following questions might be useful.

- Were the audience taken on a journey?
- Did the performance make sense to the audience?
- Did anyone in the audience laugh out loud, cry or get up and walk out?
- Did anything distract from the impact of my performance or design?
- What key feedback did we receive directly from the audience?

Now try this

Watch a short clip from a professional performance. Write a short paragraph evaluating why you think it had an impact on the audience.

Use the areas of reflection on this page to help you.

Improving process and the outcome

After reflecting on process and the contribution to a workshop performance, performers and designers consider **individual strengths** and areas to **improve**.

Contribution of ideas

Shaping of material

Participation in group tasks

Response to feedback

Design skills

Rehearsal skills

Areas to consider when planning improvements

Physical skills such as balance, coordination, alignment, flexibility, posture, stamina

Vocal skills such as use of pitch, tone, range, intonation, articulation, projection

Musical skills such as use of dynamics, expression, emphasis, timing, rhythm

Use of features such as performance space or props

Communicating with others in performance

Impact on the audience

Be honest

Considering individual strengths and areas to improve is an important part of the process of contributing to a workshop performance, whether a performer or designer is new to the industry or is highly experienced.

☑ Don't be shy about your strengths – this is not showing off! Everyone has strengths and this is your chance to comment on your best achievements during the process leading up to performance, and the performance itself.

☑ Equally, don't be embarrassed about any shortcomings you have. It is valuable to consider your weaknesses and how far you have progressed during the preparation period. This is part of the professional process to improve future contributions to the workshop performance.

To continually develop, performers and designers identify strengths and areas of shortcoming. This is an important part of the process of development, rehearsal and contribution to the workshop performance, resulting in specific plans for improvement.

Now try this

Choose two areas from the diagram above that you would like to improve in the development and rehearsal process or in live performance. Make a plan for how you will do this.

Your Component 3 set task

Component 3 will be assessed through a task, which will be set by Pearson. In this assessed task you will need to apply your skills and techniques creatively to a workshop performance for a selected audience. You will capture your ideas on planning, development and effectiveness of the performance or design process in a written log and an evaluation report.

Revising your skills

Your assessed task applies the essential content in Component 3. This skills section is designed to **revise skills** that might be needed in your assessed task. It uses selected content and outcomes to provide examples of ways of applying your skills, focusing on the **performance disciplines**.

Responding to a **brief** and **stimulus**
Look at a revision brief on page 53

Developing, rehearsing and contributing to a **workshop performance** that communicates creative intentions
Revise these skills on pages 70–72

Set task skills

Making **log notes** and completing an **ideas log** and a **skills log**
Revise these skill on pages 54–69

Completing an **evaluation report**
Revise this skill on pages 73–78

Workflow

The process of creating a group workshop performance might follow these steps:

- ✓ Review a brief and stimulus, relating it to a specific target audience.
- ✓ Participate in discussions and practical activities to shape and develop original material.
- ✓ Develop ideas and rehearse for performance.
- ✓ Keep records of how you developed your ideas and skills, to create an ideas log and a skills log.
- ✓ Present a workshop performance to an invited audience, performing or designing as part of a group and working well to apply skills and techniques to communicate your group's creative intentions.
- ✓ Evaluate your workshop performance through reflection on the process and performance.

Check the Pearson website

The activities and sample response extracts in this section are provided to help you to revise content and skills, focusing on the performance disciplines. **Every page will be of use to you, whatever your performance discipline.** Ask your tutor or check the Pearson website for the most up-to-date **Sample Assessment Material** and **Mark Scheme** to get an indication of the structure of the actual assessed task and what this requires of you, and for details relating to the **design disciplines**. The details of the actual assessed task may change, so always make sure you are up to date.

Now try this

Visit the Pearson website and find the page containing the course materials for BTEC Tech Award Performing Arts. Look at the latest Component 3 Sample Assessment Material and Mark Scheme for an indication of:

- the structure of your set task, and when you will receive it
- how much time you are allowed for preparation and performance
- what briefing or stimulus material might be provided to you
- any notes you might have to make, and whether you are allowed to take selected notes into your supervised assessment
- whether any activities need to be completed on a computer, any word limits, and any use of templates
- details relating to development of a workshop performance – the number of performers, designers, and roles involved, and any requirements for a digital recording.

Responding to a brief

When responding to a task brief, make sure you are clear about the requirements. Consider the **stimulus**, the **target audience** and the **purpose** for the workshop performance.

Understanding the skills required

This task brief is used as an example to show the skills you need. The content of a task will be different each year and the format may be different. Ask your tutor or check the Pearson website for details (e.g. group numbers; time for preparation and performance time). The details of the actual assessed task may change so always make sure you are up to date.

Task information

You have been asked by your local library to contribute to a book week they are hosting. They want to encourage members of the community to visit the library and develop an appreciation of reading. They are inviting local performance groups to show a short piece of work and have set the theme/stimulus for the performance as:

'Unlock your imagination'

In response to this theme/stimulus, you must work as part of a small group to create a Workshop Performance in a limited time slot that communicates ideas and creative intentions to a specific target audience to encourage them to develop an appreciation of reading.

Throughout the task you must participate in discussions and practical activities to shape and develop original material and ideas, and rehearse for the performance in a set time. You will need to keep records of how you developed your ideas and skills.

You must present your Workshop Performance to an invited audience. You will need to perform or design as part of a group and work well together, sharing ideas and applying performance or design skills and techniques in order to communicate your group's creative intentions.

At the end you will evaluate your Workshop Performance.

Make sure you **understand the brief** by reading it carefully more than once. You could underline key information to focus on key points.

Consider the **purpose** of performance when generating ideas in response to the **stimulus**, so your ideas are suitable.

Consider the type of **specific audience** carefully, so your ideas and performance target their age and needs, engaging them with your ideas and purposes.

Make the best use of the **skills of the group** as you discuss, shape, develop and rehearse ideas, activities and material for performance.

Keep notes of **your contribution** to the development of ideas and planning in response to the brief, your selection and development of skills and techniques, the rehearsal process and the way your work has been influenced by others.

Consider how best to work together to **communicate creative intentions in performance** by contributing and responding as a group, managing individual preparation and group rehearsal time, and progressing and refining your skills. If you are a designer, you must also present your ideas.

Evaluate your own contribution to the development of ideas, skills and the workshop performance in relation to the requirements of the brief.

 Links To revise initial responses to a brief, see pages 1–6, and for time management, see page 7.

Now try this

Use the above guidance on different stages of the task to make an outline plan of how you would manage each stage and the time to meet deadlines.

Check the BTEC Tech Award page of the Pearson website for details of your assessed task, timings, number of performers and designers, choices of disciplines.

Ideas log notes 1

As you prepare, make focused **notes** in relation to your **ideas log**. They should clearly show your individual contribution to the interpretation of the brief, and the exploration and development of ideas and planning in response to the brief. For what you should consider in your ideas log see page 58. The extracts from notes below are by an actor in response to the brief on page 53.

Sample notes extract

Target audience and purpose selected

- Performance suitable for children aged 6–10 and accessible for their parents/carers.
- Purpose: to entertain and inform.

Sample notes extract

Concept of performance in response to brief

- Looked up definitions of 'imagination'. Group definition: the creative and inventive ability to form ideas, images or concepts in our minds of something not real or not physically present to our senses.
- Agreed: make the audience use their imagination.
- Visited children's section of local library and explored non-fiction, fiction, educational books. Everyone brought in a book aimed at children aged 6–10 that included imaginary characters. Each gave 2-min summary of story and characters. Brainstormed which ones good for adapting and why, and voted on most suitable. Chose *The Little Prince* by Antoine de Saint-Exupéry. Key quotation (fox): 'You only see clearly with your heart. The most important things are invisible to the eyes.'
- Our performance: make the invisible real.
- Our impact on audience: emotional response to encourage reading the book afterwards.

Sample notes extract

Style of performance in response to brief

- Use storytelling and narration to make sure the children understand the story.
- Use group strengths of physical theatre to help children use their imaginations.
- I suggested including puppetry because young children respond well to puppets. Someone suggested using mime to impress the children. I developed the idea further of some mime being presented like magic illusions.

Preparatory notes

You may be allowed to take some of your preparatory notes into your supervised assessment time. If so, there may be restrictions on the length and type of notes that are allowed. Check with your tutor or look at the most up-to-date Sample Assessment Material on the Pearson website for information. Details of the assessment may change, so always make sure you are up to date.

Using bullet points and headings means that your notes will be **clear** and **focused**.

The **audience** and **purpose** are clearly noted, along with how individuals in the group have explored, investigated and shared initial ideas in response to the requirements of the brief.

The notes show that the **brief** has been understood, and how ideas for the performance have taken the brief into consideration.

Making notes on what you did and why you did it helps to demonstrate that you have **clear objectives** when developing your work.

Now try this

Choose a performance where you have responded to a brief. Create brief bullet points that log your ideas for the target audience, purpose, concept and style.

Ideas log notes 2

These extracts from ideas log notes are from an actor in a group, in response to the brief on page 53.

Sample notes extract

- I like how Handspring Puppet Company make characters using objects found around the house, e.g. colanders and wooden spoons.
- I want to use the group movement skills of Complicité and Frantic Assembly, with everyone stopping and moving at the same time.
- Steven Berkoff uses the body to become other animals and objects. I think that will help with showing the fox, the flowers and the snake.
- I want to include some mime skills like those used by Theatre Ad Infinitum in *Translunar Express*.

Note how these ideas relate to practical exploration of the **work of others**, and how to use or adapt these ideas in performance.

Sample notes extract

Resources needed (development and performance)

- We set deadlines for writing and blocking each scene (everyone responsible for one scene each). Script for my scene lasted 2 minutes. Used dialogue for the fox, narrator and prince. Included stage directions and blocking so everyone knows what to do and where to stand.
- We focused on what we could find or make because we have a limited budget and want to encourage the audience to use their imagination. We made a rule of one item such as a prop for each of our characters (we all play more than one role).

You will need to set **deadlines** to ensure the performance is ready within the timescale.

Make sure that you organise realistic and achievable **resources** needed in relation to your ideas.

Sample notes extract

Individual contribution to exploration and development of ideas

- I developed characters of the fox, the drunkard and the narrator. I suggested a hat for the fox and added fox ears. This led to a decision that we all wear hats.
- I suggested sound effects made with our voices, bodies and found objects, to unlock audience imagination.
- I asked another performer to watch my scene and tell me what it looked like. I did the same for them. Good to develop work together, share responsibilities and collaborate to make the work the best we could.
- I helped with making a rehearsal schedule and set a deadline for learning lines.

If you are playing more than one character, note how using a **prop** for each one can help make the character clear to the audience.

Remember to log your **own contribution** as you make notes for your ideas log.

Now try this

Choose a performance you have been involved in. Make some brief bullet notes on your individual contribution to developing ideas in response to the brief.

You could use the headings above to help focus the notes.

Skills log notes 1

As you prepare, make focused **notes** in relation to your **skills log**. Clearly show your selection and development of skills, contribution to the rehearsal process and use of the influence of others. For a summary of what you should consider in your skills log, see page 60. The extracts from notes below are from a dancer in response to the brief on page 53.

Making notes

When preparing and making focused bullet notes for your ideas and skills logs, remember these points:

- ✓ Use headings such as the ones on pages 54–57 so you have notes on important areas.
- ✓ Make sure your notes relate to the brief and your specific target audience and purpose.
- ✓ Be specific in your notes about your aims and objectives – what you did and why.
- ✓ Give examples of your own contribution and the ways you worked together as a group.
- ✓ Show how you refined your ideas, skills and techniques to engage the audience.

You can see how the notes on pages 54–57 capture areas that need to be included in the ideas and skills logs on pages 58–69. See pages 58, 64 and 69 for particular examples.

Sample notes extract

Target audience and purpose selected

- Performance suitable for teenagers aged between 15–18 (leaving school and going to sixth form or college).
- Purpose: to entertain and raise awareness of issues through using the young adult science-fiction book *Divergent* by Veronica Roth, which would appeal to this audience and get them interested in reading.

Be specific about the **target audience** in your notes. Teenagers range from 13–19 years old, and they are very different at different ages.

Sample notes extract

My role in performance

- Dauntless (the brave faction from the book *Divergent*).
- Divergent (a person who embodies all factions: Dauntless, Amity, Erudite, Abnegation and Candor).

Describe who you are in your notes. You may have many roles or just one.

Sample notes extract

Skills and techniques I selected

- Strength and control – using acrobatics such as cartwheels and walking on my hands for Dauntless.
- Dynamics – when I am Divergent I need to show the different factions. For Abnegation (selfless), I will use smooth floorwork and for Erudite (intelligence), I will use fast movement led by the head.

Note the **skills and techniques** most important to you in your performance role. Here, to show the character of being brave, lots of acrobatics are being used. The performer selected strength, knowing they need this to be able to do the required movements.

Now try this

Choose a performance you have been involved in. Make some brief bullet notes on how you selected your skills and techniques for performance.

Skills log notes 2

These extracts from skills log notes are from a musical theatre performer, in response to the brief on page 53.

Sample notes extract

Target audience and purpose selected:

- Performance suitable for pre-school children (aged 2–5) and their parents/guardians and wider family.
- Purpose is to entertain and inform.

> You should show how your skills and techniques meet the needs of your **target audience** and **purpose**.

Sample notes extract

How I developed skills and techniques for performance

- Interpretation – I developed a range of facial expressions to show the innocence, excitement and surprise of my child character. I investigated how children are presented in performance and refined characteristics by using the video on my phone.
- Physical skills – to develop my character, I observed the energy of children in different emotions and how they communicate. I built these into my movements, stage presence and interaction with other performers.

> Note the **specific** skills and techniques you develop, your investigations, and how you refine skills and techniques.

> Working with **other performers** is important.

Sample notes extract

My individual contribution to the rehearsal process

- Found and adapted a suitable song. Ensured it told a simple story and had a repetitive chorus that pre-school children would understand and enjoy.
- Worked on the song with the group and taught simple harmony for the chorus. Kept time using a tambourine and to give impact at the end.
- Developed my child character and ways to communicate the relationship when working with a partner.

> Note how your **individual contribution** in rehearsals develops the group's skills and techniques to meet the brief and engage the target audience.

Sample notes extract

How the work of others influenced my development of skills and techniques

- Structure of our piece is influenced by jukebox and song book musicals.
- Skills and techniques influenced by the way that actors play children e.g. *Blood Brothers*.
- Performance influenced by pantomime and children's theatre, e.g. speaking directly to audience and involving them.

> Note the specific ways that the **work of others** influences the development of skills and techniques. Note brief examples of how they are included in your performance.

Now try this

Choose a performance you have been involved in. Make some brief bullet notes on how you developed your skills and techniques for performance.

Acting ideas log 1

When completing your ideas log, clearly show your individual contribution to the interpretation of the brief, and the exploration and development of ideas and planning in response to the brief. The extracts from an ideas log below are in response to the brief on page 53.

Sample response extract

We selected children aged 6–10 as our target audience. The performance needs to be suitable for them, along with their parents and guardians. Our purpose is to both entertain and inform. We want to inspire the audience to visit the library to read more and respond imaginatively to stories.

These extracts show how notes made for an ideas log, such as those on page 54, can be used to complete an ideas log.

The selection of **target audience** is clear. The log shows how the ideas were decided on by the group and relate to the brief and the chosen audience.

Ideas log for all disciplines

When completing your ideas log, consider how you will provide information that includes:

- ✓ the concept and style of performance
- ✓ your target audience
- ✓ the resources needed (during development and performance)
- ✓ your contribution to the exploration and development of ideas
- ✓ how the work of others has influenced your ideas.

Sample response extract

Our concept in response to the brief is to provide inspiration for children to borrow books, take them home and bring the stories to life. After defining imagination, we investigated suitable books from the library as a group. We voted for *The Little Prince* by Antoine de Saint-Exupéry. One of the key ideas is from the fox: 'You only see clearly with your heart. The most important things are invisible to the eyes.' Our performance is going to focus on making the invisible real, and making the audience have an emotional response to the performance.

The idea for the **concept** for the performance is clear. The quotation from the chosen book links the concept to the **stimulus** to 'Unlock your imagination'.

Having clear ideas on what you want your **audience to experience** helps decision-making about what to include in your performance.

Sample response extract

When looking at the brief and the group's skills, we chose the idea of using physical theatre as our style for narrating the story. This would help children use their imaginations and understand the story. I suggested including the idea of puppetry because young children respond well to puppets. Someone suggested using mime and I developed the idea further of some mime being presented like magic illusions. These ideas would help transform the invisible into reality.

The ideas for the **style** of performance link to the brief, the audience and the concept. They take into account the skills of the group and the **resources** that are needed.

Now try this

Choose a performance you have been involved in. Complete a paragraph of an ideas log on the style of performance you chose, and why.

Acting ideas log 2

These extracts give examples of an ideas log from an actor. They relate to the notes for the ideas log on page 55, and some further notes the student made.

Sample response extract

In a version of *A Midsummer Night's Dream* we saw, the character of Puck is created by lots of performers holding together objects from a garage (the mechanics). We agreed that we would make the character of the Little Prince from found objects, and no one person would play him. This would show that he is an imaginary character that can appear and disappear quickly, as if by magic.

Your ideas log should show how the **work of others** has influenced your ideas in a clear and specific way that relates to the brief and the stimulus.

Sample response extract

In the play *Things I Know To Be True*, the characters all take it in turns to narrate their scenes. I suggested that we all do the same – we have our own scenes and we introduce and narrate them to the audience. This would mean we are responsible for the scene.

The use of narration will engage children aged 6–10. Make sure that your ideas are chosen with your **target audience** in mind.

Sample response extract

Complicité do groupwork exercises to get everyone working and moving as one. I suggested we could do this for the birds that carry the prince from his planet, and that we copy how starlings all fly together in the evening before roosting.

The idea is relevant and engaging. It shows the **influence on ideas** for the group working together in performance.

Sample response extract

We decided not to use sound effects and instead to make the sounds using our bodies, our voices and some simple household props. We chose sounds we wanted to make. We made the sound of a small plane with our voices, and I directed it to include an increase in volume and pitch when the plane crashes.

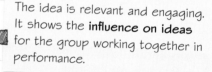

When logging **individual contribution** to the exploration and development of ideas, give examples of when you took the lead and gave direction. Alongside good teamwork, these are vital skills when creating performance material with others.

Sample response extract

We got a sheet and some torches, and tried to make shadow puppets using our hands and fingers. I taught everyone how to make a lamb shadow puppet.

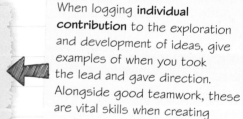

You should take responsibility for not only your own development of ideas but also for the **ideas of the group**. You might be able to develop and **provide** positive feedback on another student's work.

Now try this

Use the notes on **resources** from the middle of page 55 to write an ideas log entry for the resources needed for the development and performance.

Acting skills log 1

When completing your skills log, clearly show your selection and development of skills, contribution to the rehearsal process and use of the influence of others. The extracts from a skills log below are in response to the brief on page 53.

Sample response extract

Our group chose skills and techniques that would engage our target audience of children aged 6–10, and their parents/guardians. Skills and techniques were also chosen to meet our purpose to entertain, inform and inspire the audience to visit the library and unlock their imagination in a book.

Skills log for all disciplines

When completing your skills log, consider how you will provide information that includes:

- ☑ your role in contributing to the workshop performance
- ☑ the skills and techniques you selected
- ☑ how you developed your skills and techniques for your contribution
- ☑ your contribution to the rehearsal process
- ☑ how the work of others has influenced your development of skills and techniques.

Sample response extract

I play the roles of the narrator, drunkard and fox in the performance. I also make sound effects throughout the performance using my voice, body and objects. I am puppeteer for the prince and the lamb. With the other performers, I play the wall, the plane, a planet, the sun, the desert and the well.

These extracts give examples of a skills log from an actor in a group.

Be very specific about your **roles in the performance**, including details of the character(s) you play and any other responsibilities you have during the performance.

Sample response extract

All the skills and techniques I selected are imaginative and creative, or require the audience to use their imagination: physical theatre, mime, puppetry, ensemble work and storytelling.

Be specific about the **skills and techniques** that you selected and developed. Show how they relate to the brief, the target audience and your purpose for the performance.

Sample response extract

We needed to make each character clear and distinct so that the audience would be able to recognise them. The narrator will introduce each scene and the characters involved, but the character's voice needs to be unique. We don't want to confuse our audience.

Sample response extract

The narrator is the only character who speaks directly to the audience. We all play the narrator at different times in the play, so we included some choral speaking to show we were all the same character. The book author was a French pilot, so I found clips on YouTube of French people speaking in English, to copy how they pronounced words.

Give examples of the **range** of skills and techniques you use. Here the focus turns to vocal skills and explains the reason for the choices and how they were developed.

Now try this

Choose a performance you have been involved in. Complete a paragraph of a skills log on the techniques and skills you used to make a character clear for your audience.

Acting skills log 2

These extracts from a skills log are from an actor in response to the brief on page 53.

Sample response extract

I suggested that we all decide on an outline of our character, so it would be instantly recognisable. During a run-through of my scene I would shout 'stop' at any time and everyone would freeze. This was to make sure we were all creating clear stage images at all times. It also reflects the use of images in the book to illustrate what is happening.

*Refer to your individual contribution to the rehearsal process. Explain **why** and **how** you developed the skills and techniques you selected for performance, e.g. how you learned and adapted them.*

Sample response extract

We all had the chance to do a warm-up and I did the seven states of tension. Everyone had to pick one of their characters and decide on which state of tension, and keep this state for the whole rehearsal. It was effective, because if anyone lost focus they were reminded about their tension state by everyone else.

*Make sure that **each member** of the group contributes during rehearsals. This means that you should arrange with your group that everyone has the chance to put forward ideas and be heard.*

Sample response extract

We used the Complicité exercises in ensemble work to develop our movement and vocal work, moving or speaking at the same time. I made us slow it down as we were talking too quickly, and you couldn't hear what we were saying. This helped us be clearer and keep a strong rhythm.

*Show how the **work of others** has influenced your development of skills and techniques. This might include works of others studied in Components 1 and 2.*

Sample response extract

I developed the fox character by looking at Gregor's transformation into a beetle in *Metamorphosis* – each section of the body transforms from human to insect. I decided on the key elements of the fox's appearance – on all fours (hands and knees), tail (I bent my left leg from the knee and wagged it), body length and neck (I straightened my back and stuck my neck forward), ears and pointy nose (I stuck ears on a hat and pursed my lips). I watched some recordings of wild and tame foxes to understand how they behave, so I could copy this in my performance (the fox is tamed by the prince).

*Be **specific** about the influence on the skills and techniques you develop in relation to your role and performance.*

Now try this

Choose a performance you have been involved in. Complete a paragraph of a skills log on how you developed two key skills or techniques for performance.

Dance ideas log 1

When completing your ideas log, clearly show your individual contribution to the interpretation of the brief, and the exploration and development of ideas and planning in response to the brief. See page 58 for a summary of what you should consider in your ideas log. The extracts from an ideas log below are in response to the brief on page 53.

Sample response extract

We selected teenagers aged 15–18 as our target audience. Our purpose is to both entertain and raise awareness of issues when leaving school and going to sixth form or college.

The selection of target **audience** and **purpose** is clear and specific.

Sample response extract

We chose to use the book *Divergent* by Veronica Roth. It is a young adult science-fiction book and would appeal to this audience. We are showing the ideas in the book to get teenagers interested in reading them. We want to entertain but also inform the audience about what to expect in the book.

The log shows how the ideas for the **concept** relate to the brief and target audience.

Sample response extract

We want to show the imaginary world of the different factions (Dauntless, Amity, Erudite, Abnegation and Candor) and how we can't be put in a box. So we are all Divergent. This will appeal to the target audience as people our age are often stereotyped, and we feel like we have to fit a category. We are going to use a projector and some images to help give some extra information to the audience. Our target audience will like the use of multimedia.

Ideas for the concept are **developed** and relate to the brief and to engaging their target audience. This student has explained their idea for performance and use of the projector.

Sample response extract

We are going to begin with someone opening the book and starting to read it. This will show we are all in their imagination and coming out of the book. The performance ends with the book being closed. The person will be one of us, video recorded and played on the projector.

Ideas for the concept are **structured**. An idea is identified to start and end the performance, which directly relates to the brief.

Sample response extract

We have chosen a contemporary dance style because contemporary choreography has more flexibility in the movements we can use. Each faction is going to have its own performance quality and motif/movement phrases which show what they are like.

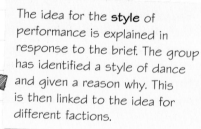

The idea for the **style** of performance is explained in response to the brief. The group has identified a style of dance and given a reason why. This is then linked to the idea for different factions.

Now try this

Choose a performance you have been involved in. Complete a paragraph of an ideas log on your contribution to the interpretation of the brief.

Dance ideas log 2

These extracts give examples of an ideas log from a dancer in response to the brief on page 53.

Sample response extract

We have been inspired by *Ghost Dances* and how songs represent a type of person. Because we have five factions we are going to have five sections, each one showing the quality of each faction. We are going to think about linking sections like in *Ghost Dances*. The person representing the faction will start to change their movement to another faction, and they will be punished for doing so, as in *Ghost Dances*.

Show how the **work of others** has influenced your ideas. Here, a link is made to a specific dance piece choreographed by Christopher Bruce. The student identifies how the structure of Bruce's choreography has inspired their own structure.

Sample response extract

To develop our ideas, we need a large rehearsal space and dance clothing. We need computer access for research, for editing and organising the PowerPoint, and a projector. We also need access to music, editing equipment for the soundtrack and a sound system to play music. For our final performance we need black clothing, someone to run the music and someone to run the projector.

Identify the **resources** you need for development and performance. Here, the student has identified the different resources needed to develop and perform the final piece. The resources include people to run the sound and the projector. You will need to show that you have thought about what you need on the day for everything to run smoothly.

Sample response extract

I contributed to exploration by suggesting the book *Divergent*. I contributed the movement for Dauntless by researching bravery and risk-taking. I used images of different risk-taking sports to come up with some movements. I also helped others in creating their faction movement, e.g. Nicole was having trouble with Amity, so I suggested that Peaceful is still, with no fast movements.

You need to show your **individual contribution** to the development of ideas. Here, the student identifies their own contribution in choreographing their faction movement. They explain how their ideas developed through investigation and images. You should show how you contribute ideas by **helping others**, and state exactly what that contribution was.

Sample response extract

I helped develop the linking sections by suggesting we all played the part of keeping each other in our place. We did an improvisation where Amy experimented with introducing movements from the other factions. When she started doing the Abnegation movement, Joshua went over and picked her up off the floor. We thought it was good and I suggested exploring more contact work.

Here, the individual contribution of suggesting an improvisation is logged, highlighting action that came from it, how it inspired them and how that was taken forward, here exploring contact work.

Now try this

Choose a performance you have been involved in. Complete a paragraph of an ideas log on how the work of others has influenced your ideas.

Dance skills log 1

When completing your skills log, clearly show your selection and development of skills, contribution to the rehearsal process and use of the influence of others. See page 60 for a summary of what you should consider in your skills log. The extracts from the skills log below are in response to the brief on page 53.

Sample response extract

For our target audience of teenagers aged between 15 and 18, we need to have high energy and something interesting to say, to unlock their imagination and engage them in books such as *Divergent* by Veronica Roth.

> These extracts show how notes made for a skills log, such as those on page 56, can be used to complete a skills log.

> There is a link to the demands of the **target audience** for the skills and content needed to engage them with the stimulus.

Sample response extract

I had two roles in the performance. Dauntless (the brave faction from the book *Divergent*) and Divergent (a person who embodies all factions: Dauntless, Amity, Erudite, Abnegation and Candor). For Dauntless, I selected skills and techniques that require strength and control, e.g. acrobatics such as cartwheels and walking on my hands. These also require stamina for sustaining high energy levels. For Divergent, I need to show contrast in my dynamics to reflect each faction. For Abnegation (selfless) I will use smooth floorwork, and for Erudite (intelligence) I will use fast movement led by the head. When I become Divergent because I want to be myself, I use facial expressions to show I am scared of being taken away, and to show anger and frustration at being put back into my box.

> The number of **roles**, along with characteristics and skills for the roles, are clearly identified. The explanation of why they have been chosen is linked to the dance idea. Each skill or technique selected is developed through the rehearsal process.

Sample response extract

Strength and control were developed by weightlifting at the gym and warm-ups, e.g. press-ups and tricep-dips for upper body strength, squats for strong legs, and sit-ups and the plank for a strong core. Stamina was developed by aerobic work, e.g. running around the room, touching the floor, jumping and rolling, to raise our heartbeats. I also took up running.

> Give details as to what you did to **get better** at your skills and techniques. These can be developed in the rehearsal room or in your own time.

Sample response extract

Dynamics were developed by watching recordings of how we were performing each movement. We used practice and repetition to make sure we showed enough contrast. We also asked our acting friends to run a workshop on facial expression. They developed our ability to show emotion in natural and extreme ways, giving feedback.

> Each skill is shown to be developed using different **strategies**, such as specific exercises, reviewing recordings of performance in rehearsal or even getting a free workshop.

Now try this

Choose a performance you have been involved in. Complete a paragraph of a skills log on two key skills and techniques you have selected and developed.

Dance skills log 2

These extracts give examples of a skills log from a dancer in response to the brief on page 53.

Sample response extract

I led some of the warm-ups and gave ideas for different exercises that would help us get better. I gave the idea for the strength-building exercises, as I said that we all had to show Dauntless at some point in the dance and we need it to be impressive.

Identify your **individual contribution** to the rehearsal process. Give examples of what you did.

Sample response extract

I gave feedback to the group when we watched video recordings of ourselves in rehearsals. I did this in a positive way so that everyone felt supported. I told Amy she needed to whip her head more in the posé turn, to show off how intelligent she is by using her head a lot.

Show how you **worked together as a group** and give examples of how you supported others in developing the skills of the group.

Sample response extract

I attended all my sessions and helped Emily as she was struggling to get to all the rehearsals. I made sure I did extra activities to get myself fitter in time for the performance, such as running and going to the gym.

Think about your **contribution** as a performer and show how managing yourself successfully enabled you to contribute effectively.

Sample response extract

Christopher Bruce uses professional dancers who are very strong and precise. They make lifts and contact work look easy. We wanted to be able to do this safely and make it look easy, so we had to build our strength. We also liked how his work focuses on society, and this book does that. We also thought how he structured his piece *Ghost Dances* was really effective, and this inspired us to use this in our piece.

Show how the **work of others** influenced your development of skills and techniques in performance. Here, the work of Christopher Bruce inspired strength, precision and the effortless ability of the dancers making contact work look easy. The structure of the work also reflects the influence of others, and links back to the brief.

Now try this

Choose a performance you have been involved in. Complete a paragraph of a skills log on how the skills and techniques you have selected and developed have been influenced by the work of others, in response to the brief.

Musical theatre ideas log 1

When completing your ideas log, clearly show your individual contribution to the interpretation of the brief, and the exploration and development of ideas and planning in response to the brief. See page 58 for a summary of what you should consider in your ideas log. The extracts from an ideas log below are in response to the brief on page 53.

Sample response extract

We selected pre-school children aged 2–5 as our target audience. We also want to target their parents/guardians and other family members, e.g. older siblings and grandparents. Our purpose is to entertain and inform about reading for pre-school children, engaging them to unlock their imaginations.

The **target audience** and **purpose** is specific and clear in relation to the brief and the stimulus.

Sample response extract

We will use music, song and dance to bring characters from popular children's books to life. We visited our local library and looked at books in the pre-school section. We borrowed some with strong central characters that could have lives outside their story. The character I have chosen is Bernard from the book *Not Now, Bernard* by David McKee.

The **concept** of performance in response to the brief is clear.

The group and individuals have **investigated** and explored source materials (children's books) and made clear decisions in response to their investigations.

Sample response extract

Our musical will allow characters from the books to talk directly to the audience about what fun reading is. The characters will also tell children how they love being taken home when their book is borrowed. We will teach children about what a library is and engage them with reading in the library and at home.

There are **clear aims** about how the audience will experience and learn from the performance. This is helpful when making decisions about what to include.

Sample response extract

We will create a 'mini' book musical. It will have a story and characters, and the songs will mark the key points in the plot.

The **style** chosen for performance is clear and purposeful. The choices relate well to the target audience.

Now try this

Choose a performance you have been involved in. Complete a paragraph of an ideas log on the exploration and development of two key ideas in response to the brief.

Musical theatre ideas log 2

These extracts give examples of an ideas log from a musical theatre performer in response to the brief on page 53.

Sample response extract

The musical *Return to the Forbidden Planet* by Bob Carlton used popular pre-existing songs that the audience would already know. The songs were linked together by the plot, just like in a book musical. The musical was also a fantasy, set on a spaceship in the future. Our musical will also use pre-existing songs, but rather than using pop and rock music, we will use existing children's songs. The book musicals of the mid-20th century have musical numbers for the chorus as well as solos and duets. We will begin and end our piece with a chorus number performed by all the characters.

This shows a good understanding of some of the **key features** of jukebox and book musicals.

The **influence** on choices for performance are clear and relate to the brief and target audience.

Sample response extract

We need the books that we chose for our characters and our own scenes based on them. I wrote a scene for my character lasting about two minutes. My scene includes a conversation between my character Bernard from *Not Now, Bernard* and Max from *Where the Wild Things Are*. Alice (who is playing Max) and I read through the scene a few times so see how it flowed, and I made some tweaks to the dialogue. We then performed it to the rest of the group to get some feedback.

Identify the **resources** you need for development and performance in relation to your ideas. Here, the books are used for reference, along with the individual scripts that have been developed.

Show how the group **worked together** to share and develop ideas.

Sample response extract

I searched online for children's songs about reading and books, and found a song about visiting a library and borrowing particular books. It inspired me to write some lyrics to mention the books and characters we have chosen to unlock the children's imagination. I used a repetitive tune and chorus to make it easy for the audience to learn.

Show your **own contribution** to the development of ideas and how they relate to the brief, the stimulus and the audience.

Now try this

Choose a performance you have been involved in. Complete a paragraph of an ideas log on how the work of others has influenced your ideas.

Musical theatre skills log 1

When completing your skills log, clearly show your selection and development of skills, contribution to the rehearsal process and use of the influence of others. See page 60 for a summary of what you should consider in your skills log. The extracts from the skills log below are in response to the brief on page 53.

Sample response extract

We selected skills and techniques to communicate a simple plot that children aged 2–5 will follow, and to perform strong characters that the children could engage with, to unlock their imaginations. Our purpose was to entertain and inform.

⬅ The skills and techniques are chosen to engage the **target audience** and achieve the **purposes** of the brief.

Sample response extract

In the performance I play Bernard, a boy whose mum is always too busy to notice him. He's eventually eaten by a big purple monster who his mum sends to bed, not noticing it isn't Bernard. I act and sing in the musical. I also wrote a scene and devised some new lyrics for a chorus song which is used at the beginning and end of the musical.

⬅ The **roles** in performance are clear in relation to acting, singing, writing a scene and devising new lyrics.

Sample response extract

To give a strong performance, I developed my skills and techniques in acting, singing in an ensemble and storytelling. My character is always interrupted by other characters and never gets listened to. I decided to use facial expressions to show how frustrated I get with this. We did some exercises in Component 2 about communicating how you feel without words. I practised my physicality and facial expressions in front of a mirror, and worked with a partner who gave me feedback.

⬅ The roles relate to the chosen **style** of 'mini-book' musical theatre, and the lyrics also relate to the **structure** of the piece. The development of skills and techniques are specific and clearly explained in relation to communication of the ideas and character.

Sample response extract

I worked on characterisation when developing my singing skills. Bernard is a little boy, so my singing style needed to fit with this. I tried to develop a soft quality to my voice to suit the character of Bernard, as he is lacking in confidence and is easily ignored.

⬅ Exercises are used to **develop skills and techniques**, drawing on learning elsewhere in the course. Be clear about how you learn and develop your skills and techniques, and how individuals and the group work together to develop them.

Sample response extract

I have a scene with Alice who plays Max from the book *Where the Wild Things Are*. We use audience participation when we argue about whose book has the best monster. We practised this using our group as the audience to give us feedback. We then adapted it and practised until it was working.

⬅ The development of skills and techniques is informed by the character in performance, practising in front of others and **adapting** in response to feedback. Be clear about how you adapt or refine your skills and techniques for your performance.

Now try this

Choose a performance you have been involved in. Complete a paragraph of a skills log on two key skills and techniques you have selected and developed.

Musical theatre skills log 2

These extracts give examples of a skills log from a musical theatre performer in response to the brief on page 53.

Sample response extract

I came up with the idea to use a song about visiting the library at the beginning and the end of the musical. Each of our characters is introduced when it is sung at the beginning. I also worked out some chords so that Jason can play the song on his guitar while we sing it. Once Jason had learned the song I taught it to the group, and we then worked out some movements to go with it.

These extracts show how notes made for a skills log, such as those on page 57, can be used to complete a skills log.

Be clear about your **individual contribution** to the rehearsal process, and show how you contribute to developing the **skills of the group** in rehearsal.

Sample response extract

My character is a lot younger than me so I looked for examples of adult actors playing children. In Component 1 we studied the musical *Blood Brothers*. I watched some recordings online and looked for how the actors behaved when playing children. I liked the way the actor playing Edward used his voice and how his posture was different to the other boys. I decided that Bernard might be quite a posh kid as well, and might behave like Edward.

Build on your work in the rest of the course to **develop skills and techniques** in your performance. Explain how you explored and investigated **the works of others** and how they influenced your development of skills and techniques, giving examples.

Sample response extract

I needed to make sure that my characterisation was consistent throughout the whole piece, not just in the bits when I was speaking. To find Bernard's singing voice I listened to the way in which my five-year-old cousin sings. I played some singing games with him and discovered that he has quite a breathy tone to his voice. Having good breath control when you are singing creates a clear and ringing tone. I was going for the opposite of this so I tried to exhale slightly as I sang to create a soft and breathy tone.

I then recorded myself and listened back, comparing it to my cousin until I got it right.

The use of characterisation is important when **developing singing skills** in musical theatre. Your character must be believable at all times, so you need to find their singing as well as their speaking voice.

Now try this

Choose a performance you have been involved in. Complete a paragraph of a skills log on how the skills and techniques you have selected and developed have been influenced by the work of others, in response to the brief.

Preparing and performing 1

As you prepare and perform your workshop performance to an invited audience, make sure you show your individual performance skills and techniques, interaction with other performers and communication of creative ideas to the audience through your role. The extracts below are from a performer's checklist in response to the brief on page 53.

Sample notes extract

For the performance I will:

- know my cues
- conduct a warm-up (vocal and/or physical)
- do focus exercises
- practise with props in the performance space
- check my own props before the start
- avoid introducing something new or changing things unless absolutely necessary.

Make sure you are **prepared and alert** so that you are in control of your performance, whatever might arise. Being prepared will increase the strength of your performance.

Performance details

Ask your tutor or check the Pearson website for details of your actual assessed performance, for example:

✓ number of performers and designers in the group

✓ time allowed for the performance

✓ any requirements for recording the performance.

Details of the assessment may change, so always make sure you are up to date.

The more you **rehearse**, the more embedded the skills and techniques will be in your performance. Consider your technical, stylistic, performance and interpretive skills, and how you use these to communicate the theme and your creative intent to your target audience.

Perform every run-through as if it's your final performance. Don't save yourself for the night. Doing your **absolute best** in every rehearsal will mean you will get better than you ever thought possible.

Nervous energy can be useful for performers as the mind and body is being prepared for the performance. **Channel your energy** and focus it on your performance.

Make sure that **every moment counts** in your performance.

Sample notes extract

Individual performance skills and techniques

For the performance I will do these tasks:

- Practise skills I find difficult. For example, remaining as still as possible once the first movement sequence is completed. It's really energetic and I sometimes lose focus and concentration when doing the freeze-frame. I need to remain in the moment and not worry about what is coming next, as when I worry I sometimes fidget.

- With the group, do a speed run of the performance material the day before. This will help to get the running order fixed in our minds so we can concentrate on practising our own performance technique.

- Be positive about the performance and supportive of others so that nerves don't affect us in a negative way.

- Keep focused throughout the performance.

Now try this

Think back to your last performance – were there any mishaps? Write down what they were, and what you could do to avoid them in future.

Preparing and performing 2

Consider the points below as you perform your piece. The extracts give examples of a performer's checklist in response to the brief on page 53.

Sample notes extract

Interaction with other performers

For the performance I will do the following:

- Be sure we trust each other. If there are areas we aren't sure about as a group, we should rehearse these before the performance. We don't want the audience to notice any mistakes.
- Make sure we know our positioning. In some parts of the performance, all performers have to move as one unit. We must know our positioning for each section and the timing of our movements.
- Take part in a group warm-up so we are working together and feeling like one team, e.g. singing a song.
- Make sure we are working together to communicate our ideas to the audience, and not just focusing on my own performance.
- Believe in my own skills and abilities, trust that my fellow performers will do the same, and demonstrate pride and confidence in the work we've created.

Workshop performance for all disciplines

When presenting your piece, consider how you will:

☑ deliver and communicate ideas through your role

☑ show your ability to communicate with others

☑ apply your skills and techniques.

Rehearse the work as much as you can so you are very familiar with it, just in case anyone misses a cue and you need to cover up the mistake.

Use a warm-up that you are familiar with in rehearsals, as it can settle your nerves and focus the group.

You are not alone in the performance. You are one performer in a group, **collaborating** towards one goal: to perform the work successfully to your audience.

You will need to be **alert** during the performance. Listen and respond to the other performers as if for the first time.

Remember your aims for this performance, who your audience is and what you want them to experience. Being **confident** in your performance can make a huge difference to what an audience will experience. The best way to gain confidence is to believe in your performance material and practise your role as much as you can.

The best professional performers will **make it look easy**, even if they are performing demanding or difficult material. You can be your own harshest critic. Make yourself proud.

Sample notes extract

Communication of creative ideas to the audience through my role

For the performance I will do the following:

- Keep the stimulus, theme and purpose of our performance in mind and remember the aims and objectives. Be clear and precise about the ideas we want to communicate to the audience and what we want them to feel.
- Keep the flow going, without stopping or breaking the action. If something goes wrong, stay confident and remain in role so the audience believes in our performance. Imagine watching myself in performance and expect to see a confident, assured delivery. Perform with energy and commitment, providing the audience with the best performance I can.

Now try this

Create your own checklist for your workshop performance, reflecting your own discipline and role.

You could use the headings and notes on page 72 to guide you.

Workshop performance debrief

It is useful to debrief immediately after your performance. Write notes and analyse audience feedback and any recordings. This will help you to evaluate your performance while it is fresh in your mind. The extracts below are from a performer's checklist of debrief questions in response to the brief on page 53.

Sample notes extract

How the outcome met the requirements of the brief
- Which specific target audience did we choose, and why?
- How did our work encourage the audience to develop an appreciation of reading?
- Did our work meet the theme 'unlock your imagination'? In what ways?
- What style, structure and form did we use, and why?

When you debrief after the workshop performance, refer also to earlier notes. Reflecting on your suggestions and ideas in the **planning stages and rehearsals** can make a real difference when evaluating your work.

Sample notes extract

The development process
- What investigation did we do, and how did it contribute to the work?
- What ideas did we contribute during the development of the work?
- Did we find it easy or difficult to communicate ideas with our group?
- What decisions did we make, and how did they affect the process?
- What personal skills and techniques did we develop and demonstrate?

Being an active member of the group, making positive contributions regularly, and being reliable and committed are all vital skills when developing performance material. When debriefing after the performance, it's an opportunity to discuss the **significance of your impact** during the whole process.

Sample notes extract

The performance outcome
- Were our intentions clear?
- What individual and group performance skills and techniques did we use, and were they successful?
- What would we change about the performance, and why?
- What skills and techniques would we want to develop for further performances?

Include **feedback from the audience** when reviewing your performance. For example, you could hold a question and answer session after the performance, use an anonymous questionnaire, or talk with the audience afterwards.

Along with your own reflections, ask others for honest feedback in the development process and performance outcome. Watch clips of rehearsals and performance to **analyse** how you communicate and perform with others.

Sample notes extract

Key strengths of my work and areas for further development
- How did I use my preparation time?
- How did I practise my roles and ensure I was focused and reliable in group rehearsals?
- Which ideas did I contribute, and how did the group and audience respond to them?
- Which skills and techniques were effective, and did any need more refinement?
- Did I sustain total focus, commitment and positive attitude in performance?

Now try this

Choose a performance you have been involved in. Make notes that review the performance outcome of your piece.

Acting evaluation 1

When writing your acting evaluation report, make sure you show your ability to evaluate your own contribution to the development of ideas, skills and the workshop performance. The extracts from an evaluation below are made in response to the brief on page 53.

Sample response extract

We spent time exploring the brief, so our performance best met the requirements. Our target audience was children aged 6–10, with a purpose to entertain and inform. We wanted to inspire them to use their local library to get reading and unlock their imaginations. We chose books for our work they could borrow and read. We chose to interpret the books in a highly imaginative way to encourage them to use their imaginations when watching the performance.

Evaluating performance for all disciplines

When writing your report, consider how you will evaluate your individual and group contribution to:

- ✓ how the outcome met the requirements of the brief
- ✓ the development process
- ✓ the performance outcome
- ✓ key strengths of your work
- ✓ areas for further development.

These extracts give examples of an evaluation report from an actor.

Reflect on the **original intentions** of your performance in response to the brief, and decide if you met the requirements.

Sample response extract

We decided to use mime so the audience would have to imagine the objects. We also chose physical theatre where we would 'become' objects, animals and landscapes, so the audience would have to use their imaginations. We only referred to the book a little bit, to encourage the children to read it and find out what happens.

Sample response extract

We investigated books at our local library, and each person chose one for the age group that was magical or creative fiction. We presented a summary for each other, with ideas on how it could be transformed into performance. This allowed us all to demonstrate our investigation skills and use our imaginations for interpreting a story into a theatrical performance.

Consider the **investigation** you did for this work, and how different ideas from yourself and the group were explored and used in the process of development.

Sample response extract

There can be many good ideas in a group but no one making decisions, so we had a leader for each scene. In my scene, I suggested using a hat to indicate the central character, so the audience knows who they are and their status. We developed this by using the hat idea in all scenes so it's clear who the audience should focus on. For sound effects, I suggested using our voices, bodies and 'props' (such as paper plates and wooden spoons) to show children they can use objects around the house imaginatively to create new worlds and characters.

Think about your **own contribution** during rehearsals. Were you a good team player? Evaluate your contributions to the content, shape and form of your performance material, and consider what others did to make this a success.

Now try this

Choose a performance you have been involved in. Write a paragraph that evaluates your own contribution in developing one of the ideas for performance.

Acting evaluation 2

These extracts give examples of an actor's evaluation report in response to the brief on page 53. For a summary of what you should consider when evaluating your performance, see page 73.

Sample response extract

Our main aims were to unlock the imaginations of the audience, to entertain and inform them. I feel that, based on their reactions, our performance outcome was successful. For example, they laughed at the character entrances, lines and interactions that we designed to be funny. They joined in when we asked them questions about how to draw an imaginary snake who has eaten an elephant, and one child screamed when we recreated the snake's movements.

Evaluate the **performance outcome** and give examples to show how you had your intended effect on the audience.

Sample response extract

We practised our storytelling performance techniques, such as clarity and musicality of the voice, so we were not monotonous and boring to the audience. We were as physically expressive as possible. We carried out a question and answer session with the audience, did an anonymous questionnaire, and spoke to some of the children and parents, who gave us feedback. They wanted to know more about what happens to the Little Prince in the story, so we feel we achieved what we intended.

Show how far the **skills and techniques** you developed achieved the performance outcome. You could use different methods to gather **audience feedback** and include it in the evaluation of the performance outcome.

Sample response extract

I was committed to bringing key strengths to the work throughout the process. I learned my lines and movements quickly so the rehearsals went smoothly, with good progress. I was a reliable group member, on time and meeting deadlines. I directed my scene by explaining the context, the motivations and possible ways for other performers to interpret their characters and deliver lines. I accepted the opinions of others and changed my first ideas to incorporate theirs. I practised mime skills and choral work to ensure the audience would experience an entertaining and imaginative performance.

Evaluate the strengths of your work and **your contributions** throughout the process. Provide honest and clear examples of your positive contributions to the performance work, including a focus on your personal skills and how you interacted with the group.

Sample response extract

When considering areas for further development, we would focus on ensuring that all cues (entrances, exits and cue biting) were sharper. When analysing the performance recording, some of the group were slightly behind, and a bit unsure. We would refine our choral work through commitment to group rehearsals. Some characters seemed underdeveloped, shown in the voice of the performer not being loud and clear. We would rehearse these characters to be as big and expressive as the rest. To meet the aim of unlocking the imagination of the audience, we need to ensure the standard of performance enables this.

Evaluate areas for **further development**. Consider the skills and techniques you would develop if you were to perform this work again. Include the response of the audience and talk to them afterwards. A questionnaire can be a good, anonymous method of capturing feedback.

Now try this

Choose a performance you have been involved in. Write a paragraph that evaluates your contribution to the development of skills for rehearsal and performance.

Dance evaluation 1

When writing your dance evaluation report, make sure you show your ability to evaluate your own contribution to the development of ideas, skills and the workshop performance. For a summary of what you should consider when evaluating your performance, see page 73. The extracts from an evaluation below are made in response to the brief on page 53.

Sample response extract

Our final performance of *Divergent* was really effective in meeting the requirements of the brief. In the question and answer session at the end of the performance, many in the audience said they wanted to read the book now. This links with the brief, because we encouraged the audience to go to the library to get the book out.

◀ Make **evaluative comments** about your piece and state why it met the brief. Link to the requirements of the brief to show that you had this in mind all along. You could include feedback from the audience gathered from a post-performance question and answer session, an anonymous questionnaire, or talking with the audience after the performance.

Sample response extract

The projection of Amy opening the book and us walking forward from the projection made it look like we were characters in the book and showed us inside Amy's imagination. We were able to show that the book unlocked her imagination and we were in her imagination.

◀ Give examples that help evaluate and show **how the outcomes met the requirements of the brief**.

Sample response extract

When we were creating the movement for the different factions, some factions were easy to create for and others were not. I think I had an easy faction (Dauntless), and I was able to contribute my movement phrases quite quickly. Erudite and Abnegation were also easy. But Candor and Amity were quite difficult because they were Honest and Peaceful, which are really difficult to show in movement. We all pitched in here and found that it was easier to contrast them against the other movements. Working as a team was really important here.

◀ Make evaluative comments about **the development process**, and give details from what happened to help explain it.

◀ Evaluate your **own contribution** and how you worked together as a **group** within the development process.

Now try this

Choose a performance you have been involved in. Write a paragraph that evaluates your own contribution in developing one of the ideas for performance.

Dance evaluation 2

These extracts give examples of a dancer's evaluation report in response to the brief on page 53. For a summary of what you should consider when evaluating your performance, see page 73.

Sample response extract

When we watched back a recording of our final performance, we analysed how effective we were, as if in the audience. We had all kept our focus throughout the performance. We kept in our characters and used our faces to show the emotion of each faction or the frustration we felt. However, our peaceful faces looked a little smug, so we could work on that. We did find it difficult to show this. My performance looked like I was part of a team, because we were well rehearsed and I had worked with the other dancers to make it a slick performance.

These extracts give examples of an evaluation report from a performer who is a dancer.

Evaluate the **performance outcome**. You could analyse recordings of rehearsals and performance. Don't forget to include your own contribution.

Sample response extract

In our audience questionnaires, some people said that we could all be a bit more confident in our performance. I could see why when analysing the video. We weren't projecting as much as we could, which made us look under-confident. It was like we were doing it for TV, and when the audience is far away we need to make all our movements bigger. This was mostly in our solo transitions, when we tried to show an emotion.

Use **audience feedback** in your evaluation. You could conduct a post-performance question and answer session, use anonymous questionnaires and speak to the audience after the performance. You can then use this insight to help you evaluate your performance.

Sample response extract

We showed many **key strengths** in our work throughout the process. For example, we responded to the brief and showed imagination when relating to books effectively. We considered early on how ambitious to be with contact work, as we knew we didn't have the time to be slick. We worked well together. There were no rows and so we had more time to focus on rehearsal. We all knew the steps and the structure of the work because we were well rehearsed.

Focus on the final performance and highlight what worked and what didn't work so well. You could identify your **key strengths** separately or as you go along.

In your evaluation, show how you take the **skills and abilities of the group** into account when devising, which is a key strength.

Sample response extract

We could have considered focusing on a few books instead of one, and explored the word 'imagination' through how characters from different books might interact, e.g. what would happen if Hermione Granger and Katniss Everdeen were in the same room? This might have linked to the world of books and unlocking imagination.

You can identify areas for **further development** as you go along, or separately. Here, there is evaluation of whether the original ideas could have been better, explaining what could have happened.

Now try this

Choose a performance you have been involved in. Write a paragraph that evaluates your contribution to the development of skills for rehearsal and performance.

Musical theatre evaluation 1

When writing your musical theatre evaluation report, make sure you show your ability to evaluate your own contribution to the development of ideas, skills and the workshop performance. For a summary of what you should consider when evaluating your performance, see page 73. The extracts from an evaluation below are made in response to the brief on page 53.

Sample response extract

One of the requirements of the brief was to encourage members of the community to visit the library. I think we have met this requirement as our musical showed pre-school children that the library is a fun place to visit.

Revisit the brief. Consider how your finished piece met the **requirements of the brief**.

Sample response extract

Our opening and closing song was about how much fun it is to borrow books, bring them back and then borrow new ones. We taught the chorus to the children, and some were still singing it when we spoke with the audience for feedback afterwards. Hopefully they will remember the song long after the show.

Refer to particular aspects of the performance to **support** how your work met the brief.

Sample response extract

A key moment in the development process was deciding that the characters from the books were trying to get the children to borrow their books so they could be taken home and read. This meant the characters could speak to the audience directly and allowed audience participation. Audience participation is a key feature of pantomime and other forms of family entertainment, so including it was a good decision.

Evaluate key moments in the **development process** of your performance, such as when an important decision was made, or how an aspect of the performance came together in rehearsal. Explain how these moments in the development process contributed to the success of the final performance. Use examples to illustrate your points.

Sample response extract

We decided the main song of our piece would be taught to the audience. We needed to work out the best way of doing this. At first we wanted to teach the full song to the audience, but then decided it was not a good idea because when we tried it out on a group in our class it took too long and they got confused. I suggested that we concentrate on the chorus. We then decided to break the chorus into two-bar sections, and use a call and response game to introduce the song. This worked well, as we could teach the chorus to people who didn't know the song really quickly using this technique.

Discuss any ideas that were rejected, explaining why they were not chosen. Perhaps they were inappropriate for the target audience, or maybe there wasn't enough time or resources to make them work. Evaluate your ability to **select and adapt** ideas.

Now try this

Choose a performance you have been involved in. Write a paragraph that evaluates your own contribution in developing one of the ideas for performance.

Musical theatre evaluation 2

These extracts give examples of a musical theatre performer's evaluation report in response to the brief on page 53. For a summary of what you should consider when evaluating your performance, see page 73.

Sample response extract

The final performance was a short children's musical based in a library. The decision to have a librarian as a narrator who led the audience from scene to scene was a strength of the piece. The use of narration meant the performance had a clear structure that was easy to understand for younger audience members. It was clear from the questionnaire responses that this was successful.

When evaluating the performance outcome, give examples of how the decisions you made for performance worked for your **target audience**. You could include audience feedback from a post-performance question and answer session, anonymous questionnaires and speaking with the audience after the performance.

Sample response extract

I believe I interacted well with the librarian, and the audience were really laughing at the scene when she kept ignoring me and saying 'Not now Bernard'. I felt I made good use of physicality and facial expression in that scene to show my frustration. In the songs, I performed with good intonation and accurate rhythm. I was able to use my singing voice to enhance the audience's understanding of my character. I used a soft tone but made sure that I could still be heard.

When evaluating **key strengths**, give examples of how the ideas and skills you developed engaged the audience. Evaluate your singing skills, giving specific examples.

Sample response extract

It would be great to develop our piece into a longer musical. The characters could have more scenes, showing what it is like to go home with children when they borrow books. This would further encourage children to borrow books regularly.

When suggesting areas for further development, remember to explain **how** your suggestions would improve the performance, and **why**.

Sample response extract

I would like to add more musical numbers and perhaps use a different musical motif to introduce each character. This might make the character more memorable for the children, as when we watched the performance back we felt the difference between characters could be stronger. A duet between Bernard and Max would be a great ending to the scene where they are arguing about their monsters. It could include a comedic dance routine that the monsters could join in. I think this would be popular with the children in the audience

Evaluate the different **skills and techniques** you used in performance, and how they might be developed further. You could analyse a recording of rehearsals and performance, and include your observations in your evaluation.

Now try this

Choose a performance you have been involved in. Write a paragraph that evaluates your contribution to the development of skills for rehearsal and performance.

Answers

1. Understanding a brief

Individual responses. Your ideas should include initial consideration of the following:

- target audience
- performance space
- performance discipline, skills and strengths
- structure of the work
- genre/style
- creative intentions, responding to the theme 'New beginnings' (e.g. play to entertain and celebrate newlyweds; new street dance styles; musical about immigrants to the local area; existing repertoire that could be used as inspiration e.g. short plays by David Greig, dance work by Boy Blue Entertainment, musicals by Stephen Sondheim), resources needed, timing and number of performers.

2. Responding to stimulus

Individual responses. Here are some examples of how practical activities could be used to generate ideas in response to the theme 'Stronger together or apart':

- Brainstorm the theme. You could explore existing drama, dance and musical theatre productions that relate to this theme, and how they do so.
- Find images that relate to the theme and stick them onto a large ideas sheet, which would be displayed during rehearsals to remind us.
- Improvise the theme using only physical interaction and no words.
- Find a piece of music that captures the theme and share this with the group.

3. Target audience

Individual responses, as a list or mind map. For example:

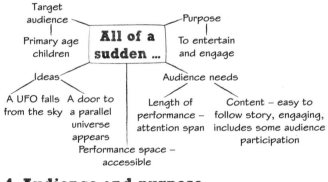

4. Audience and purpose

1 and 2 Individual responses.
3 For example:

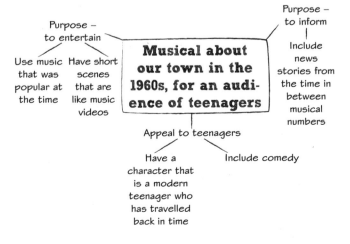

5. Performance space and staging

Individual responses. Considerations might include:

- where the audience was placed
- how close or far away they were from the performance, and reasons why
- whether the piece would look good from a different perspective
- the size of the performance space, and how that worked for the performance.

6. Using performance space

Individual responses reflecting ideas about the theme. For example, one idea of staging could be the traverse stage, because the parallel nature of the stage and audience could lend itself to using one end as the past, the centre as the present, and the other end as the future.

7. Resources

Individual responses. For example:

- **Managing resources:** We didn't have a big enough room for us all to rehearse at the same time, so we divided the movement sequences into smaller sections and decided on rehearsal times for each section.
- **Next time:** Make sure everyone sticks to the rehearsal schedule, as some groups turned up late and over-ran rehearsals, which had an impact on the next group in the rehearsal space.

8. Style

Individual responses. For example:

Style and genre: Naturalistic tragedy

Content: Salem witch trials; McCarthyism in the USA

The Crucible by Arthur Miller, Old Vic production

Structure and form: Four-act play covering events over four months

Performance style: Naturalistic costumes and set, performed in the round

9. Types of stimulus

Individual responses. Ideas might include, for example:

- teenagers driving too fast
- family journey
- being stuck and bored.

10. Theme as a starting point

Individual responses. For example:

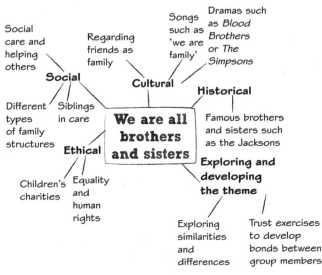

11. Issues as a starting point

Individual responses. For example:
- Issue: Fear of starting a new school/bullying after the summer holidays.
- Exploration:
  - Survey Year 7 students about their first day at secondary school.
  - Read news stories about bullying or fear of going to school.

12. Props as a starting point

Individual responses. Example workshop ideas:
- The piece of paper becomes a letter bringing bad news.
- This could lead to group or individual improvisations.
- The paper could be ripped and crumpled to show emotion of loss.

13. Setting as a starting point

Individual responses. For example:
- We used 'Is there anybody out there?' in relation to the stimulus. We wanted to explore and show how many different people might have a reason to say or think this. We listed all the different people, times and places this phrase could have been used:
  - alone in a house at night and a noise is heard in the garden
  - space exploration and the search for life on other planets
  - after an explosion
  - a late-night radio DJ.
- All examples have characters who don't know something or are looking for someone. There is tension in every example. This led us to create short scenes focusing on each example.
- We wanted our audience to feel this tension too. Our work is aimed at teenagers aged 14–16 so we decided to seat them in the round, so they could not only see the performance but also see each other's reactions. The audience would be tightly packed together so they couldn't escape. We would use recorded sound effects of weather conditions (thunder, rain, wind) to build and sustain tension, but nothing else. We wanted the audience to feel fear and tension through what they hear.

14. Existing acting repertoire

Individual responses based on the work and aspects considered. For example:

Shelagh Delaney: *A Taste of Honey*
- **Style, structure and form:** Kitchen sink drama. Two-act play. Naturalistic, i.e. realistic language, characters and actions. We learn about the characters and their histories through the words they say about each other.
- **Theatrical elements:** Naturalistic costume, setting and props.
- **Context:** Written by Delaney when she was 18. First shown in 1958 by Joan Littlewood's Theatre Workshop at Stratford East in London. Really successful with West End and Broadway versions, then made into a film. Included references to life that hadn't been shown in theatre before, such as being gay, poverty and teenage pregnancies. The main character, Jo, has lots of problems to solve throughout the play and the play ends with her in a difficult position, alone. We are not sure what will happen to her.

15. Existing dance repertoire

Individual responses based on the work and qualities considered.

16. Existing musical theatre repertoire

Individual responses based on the work and qualities considered.

17. Acting genre, style and structure

Individual responses. Some examples may include:

Naturalism:
- plot: focus on what happens and to whom
- dialogue: realistic dialogue and interaction between characters – how people talk in a particular context
- believable characters
- audience: viewing action through fourth wall (like watching real action through glass).

Epic:
- plot: focus on why and how things happen
- dialogue: performers might talk about own characters in third person, larger than life, and so on.
- exaggerated characterisation, stereotypes
- audience: performers directly address audience, reminding them they are watching a play, not to be lost in the action.

18. Dance genre, style and structure

Individual responses. Some examples are given here.
Contemporary
- Flowing dynamics (e.g. flowing, weighted, moving away from ballet, strong, controlled).
- Use of the floor (e.g. bare feet, parallel feet; mixed or developed from other styles, such as jazz or ballet; no restrictions on movement style).

Jazz dance
- Use of set jazz steps (e.g. lyrical jazz, musical theatre, Latin jazz, African jazz).
- Use of certain music or practitioner influence (e.g. Fosse, Cole and Luigi jazz styles).

Ballet
- Use of set ballet steps and different styles (e.g. classical, romantic).
- Use of narrative and different compositional structures (e.g. fairy tales, original ballet stories).

19. Musical theatre genre, style and structure

Individual responses. Some examples are given here.
Book musical
- Narrative plot – boy meets girl, boy loses girl, boy wins girl back.
- Characters – male and female leads, supporting characters, comic characters.
- Showstopper chorus numbers.

Jukebox musical
- Songs are connected to a popular artist or band.
- The plot is woven around the songs.
- Dialogue is used to link the songs together.

20. Skills and creative intentions

Individual responses reflecting your own skills and knowledge which you could bring to a performance.

21. Working as a group

Individual responses. Examples are given here.

How I contribute to the exploration or development of ideas
I like to set clear instructions for the work I am responsible for so everyone knows exactly what they have to do. Sometimes it can be difficult to understand the objective of the practical work when everyone is talking, so before we begin I will state the purpose of the exploration to make sure we are all doing the same thing.

My individual contribution to the rehearsal process
- I led some discussions in our group, making sure that everyone got a chance to express their opinions on the work we were doing. Most of the time people were happy with how it was progressing but it's really useful to share thoughts in case anyone wants to make changes.
- I make notes on A3 paper during discussions to make sure that everyone has a clear record of our decisions. I then take photos of the notes and share them with everyone.

Key strengths of my work
- I always arrived early to rehearsals and prepared everything as soon as I got there.
- I set myself deadlines for learning and practising material to make sure that I knew what I was rehearsing in the next session.

Any problems I am encountering and what I did to solve them
There are some members of the group who were either arriving as the rehearsal began, or even five minutes into it, meaning that they weren't ready or missed part of the warm-up. I took on

responsibility for sending out reminders 30 minutes before the rehearsals by phone to make sure everyone arrived on time and ready to work.

22. Influence of acting practitioners

Individual responses. Examples are given here.

Alecky Blythe

- British playwright and screenwriter.
- Founder of Recorded Delivery, a theatre company specialising in verbatim theatre.
- Most famous work is *London Road*, a musical that uses real-life interviews from a local community affected by the murders of prostitutes.

Verbatim theatre

- The writer is interested in a real-life situation or event that has happened.
- The writer interviews real people.
- The dialogue is then edited by the writer and shaped into a play.
- Edited recordings are played live to the actors through earphones during rehearsals.
- Actors listen and repeat what they hear exactly – not only the words but anything else the interviewee does, such as cough.
- The purposes are:
  - to capture exactly not only what the original person said, but how they said it
  - to examine current society by representing the thoughts and opinions of people in response to an event.

23. Influences on acting

Individual responses in relation to another practitioner. An example using Stanislavski's naturalism is given here.

Style and form

A performance influenced by Stanislavski's naturalism techniques might create meaning through:

- making the audience suspend disbelief – e.g. making it seem like the action taking place is realistic and could actually happen
- use of realistic dialogue
- use of realistic costume, setting, props, sound effects
- action taking place in one environment and not moving location
- action taking place in a limited time e.g. an afternoon or evening
- an imaginary fourth wall (like a glass wall) between performers and audience. The performers don't speak to or acknowledge the audience being in the same room.

Characters

Using Stanislavski's techniques might influence skills and techniques used with characters, such as:

- creating a protagonist, i.e. a main central character who has the main objectives of the play
- creating an antagonist who may have different, opposing objectives to the protagonist
- showing the audience many lifelike elements of the character such as use of accent, gestures and movements
- having clear objectives for everything your character says and does in the play.

Influence of techniques on an audience

Here are some examples of how the audience can be persuaded to look at the performance work in a particular way. Responses can be presented as a list or mind map:

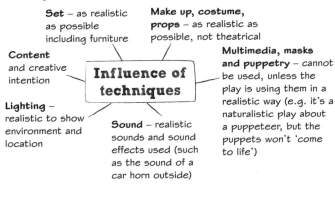

24. Influence of dance practitioners

Individual responses. For example:
I am inspired by Mia Michaels. She uses contemporary and lyrical dance styles in her choreography to get the emotion across. Her dancers need to be highly expressive and have excellent technique. I will choose a lyrical style at the end of my performance, where I want the audience to identify with the emotion of the character.

25. Influences on dance

Individual responses. Exercises/activities could include:

- isolation hip exercises, such as punches to the side, thrusts, circles, figure of eights, scoops
- travelling sequences with use of hips (e.g. walking, step ball changes).

26. Influence of musical theatre practitioners

Individual responses. For example, if considering Nancy in *Oliver!* think about how the performer communicates the following:

- **Acting skills:** Nancy is a complicated character to communicate. She has feelings for the villain, Bill Sykes, but also wants to protect Oliver.
- **Singing skills:** The song 'As Long as He Needs Me' is very challenging. The performer needs a strong and expressive singing voice.
- **Dance skills:** Some basic dance skills are needed, e.g. in 'Oom Pah Pah' and 'I'd Do Anything', but this is not a role that needs a dance specialist.

27. Influences on musical theatre

Individual responses. Examples are given here.

- **Acting:** we all have good acting skills.
- **Singing:** Anna: really good rock voice; Ben and Aanshi: good voices; Jaro: can sing in ensembles but does not like solos.
- **Dance:** Anna: good at jazz; Ben and Aanshi: good at jazz and urban; Jaro: excellent at urban dance.
- **Specialist:** Anna: can play the keyboard; Ben: good at harmonies; Aanshi: can produce vocal sound effects: Jaro: good with e.g. clapping to keep us in time.
- We have the skills needed for a book-style musical as we can all act, we can all sing to some extent and also dance. Because we have a keyboard player and most of us are good at urban dance we could also do a contemporary rock or jukebox musical.

28. Skills for young audiences

Individual responses. Two examples are given here.

Performance piece: *The Owl and the Pussycat*
Production by Kitchen Zoo, developed in partnership with ARC and The Witham.

- **Target audience:** Age 3–7 years.
- **Content:** Based on the popular children's poem of the same name written by Edward Lear. The show follows the Owl and the Pussycat who are blown out of a window in a storm. They then set out to sea on a journey to a strange land.
- **Skills to engage the audience include:** acting, singing, music performance, puppetry.
- As with many examples of theatre for children, the acting style is often heightened and performers break the fourth wall to directly engage with and involve the audience.

Performance piece: *The Lion King*, Disney

- **Target audience:** Age 6 years up.
- **Content:** The plot revolves around the young lion Simba and his friend Nala, and the story of his return from exile to challenge Scar, to end his tyranny and take his place as the rightful king in the circle of life.
- **Skills to engage the audience include:** acting, singing, music performance, puppets and masks.

- The performance includes comedy in the scenes with Timon and Pumba with appeal to a wide audience including children. Familiar songs will appeal to children who have seen the Disney film. Children will identify with the young characters Simba and Nala. The use of design features such as puppets and masks makes the piece very engaging and brings the African landscape to life.

29. Skills for wide audiences

Individual responses. Two examples are given here.
- **Theme:** The Birthday Party.
- **Initial ideas:** Murder mystery or ghost story set at a party taking place in an old country house. Could be a musical or narrative dance piece.
- **Skills:** Expressive performance skills to create a spooky or threatening atmosphere and portray characters.
- **Initial ideas:** Comedy set at an 18th birthday party where everything goes wrong.
- **Skills:** Pace, timing and physical comedy skills. Ability to work with props.

30. Vocal skills

Individual responses. Some examples may include the following.
Breathing exercises
- Breathe in for a count of three, breathe out for three, making 'hmmm' with lips gently closed.
- Pant a 'voice' and say Ha-Ha-Ha, then, on the next breath: Hee-Hee-Hee, Ho-Ho-Ho, Hey-Hey-Hey, Hi-Hi-Hi, Haw-Haw-Haw, Hoo-Hoo-Hoo.

Voice projection exercises
- Count aloud from one to ten, starting softly and then gradually increasing the loudness of your voice. But don't strain or shout.
- Count aloud from ten to one. You are trying to reach across the room with ten; by the time you get to one imagine you are whispering in someone's ear.
- Experiment with soft and loud as you count aloud.
- Then try using a line from a script.

Tongue twisters
- A proper cup of coffee in a proper copper coffee pot.
- A glowing gleam glowed grey and green.
- The feathered flush flew through the fiery flue.
- Red lorry yellow lorry/red leather yellow leather.
- She sells seashells on the sea shore.

31. Voice preparation

Individual responses. You could use include the exercises from your response to the Now try this question on page 30.

32. Physical performance skills

Individual responses. For example, ways to improve the physical skills can range from made-up activities, games and activities you have learned throughout the course, to specific fitness exercises.

33. Acting performance skills

Individual responses depending on the genre and style selected. For example:
- **In my acting piece I …** mime pushing a large object across the stage.
- **What is the problem?** Keep falling over, going too fast.
- **Why?** Not sure how heavy it is.
- **Action plan:** Push against a solid object, e.g. a wall. Notice stance, position and where the weight is held in the body. Adopt the same position without the wall. Use a mirror to see if it looks believable. Try moving forward one step slowly, showing how difficult it is to move the object, through body and facial expression. Don't rush. Rehearse and practise, adding a new step forward each time.

34. Dance performance skills

Individual responses. For example:
- **In my dance piece I …** perform a barrel turn.
- **What is the problem?** I keep falling over.
- **Why?** I'm not sure where my feet are going.
- **Action plan:** Break down the movement to just footwork. Rehearse. When confident, do footwork and spin (but no lean). Rehearse. When confident, add in the lean.

35. Musical theatre performance skills

Individual responses. For example:
- **In my song I …** am finding the leap from low to high notes difficult.
- **What is the problem?** I jump around in pitch before hitting the right note.
- **Why?** I lack confidence that I will hit the correct note.
- **Action plan:** Build confidence by improving vocal range, especially high notes, through practising scales and arpeggios. Remember to warm up and not to strain.

36. Acting group improvisation

Individual responses. When preparing your improvisation, you should consider:
- Your theme.
- Your situation: Where you are: e.g. a location such as a shop, a swimming pool.
- Your role: Who the characters are, e.g. a farmer, the prime minister.
- What you want: The characters' objectives, e.g. looking for a lost pet, wanting to make a complaint.
- What style of performance are you going to use: Consider questions such as: will it be naturalistic? Will you speak directly to the audience? Will it be fast-paced physical comedy without words?

37. Dance group improvisation

Individual responses. **Purposes** might include to:
- explore contact work
- come up with unusual formations or pathways
- explore structure
- connect with music
- find choreographic devices.

Rules can be wide-ranging and might include:
- restricting what body parts can move
- how many people performing/in the performance space
- use of levels
- use of directions
- pathways
- contact work and when it can happen.

38. Musical theatre group improvisation

Individual responses. For example, ideas about improvising to the song *Perfect* by Ed Sheeran could include:
- adding some call and response backing vocals to the end of phrases in the verses
- adding harmonies to the chorus section.

39. Developing acting style and genre

Individual responses, based on the performance chosen.

40. Developing dance style and genre

Individual responses, based on the performance chosen.

41. Developing musical theatre style and genre

Individual responses, based on the performance chosen.

42. Individual preparation

Individual responses. Here are some examples of areas to improve and appropriate exercises.

- Lack of confidence – improve by performing to new people to get used to performing.
- Poor vocal projection – improve by a vocal exercise such as 'drilling into the wall'.
- Hitting the high notes of a song – improve through a good warm-up, which includes singing scales.
- Poor flexibility making my kicks look bad – improve through hamstring and quadricep stretches in the cool-down.

43. Group rehearsals

Individual responses. Here are some examples.

1 Strengths:
- I am a good listener.
- I am well organised.

Areas for development:
- I get annoyed when others don't understand my ideas.
- I sometimes cut corners and go for the easiest option.

How I can improve:
- I need to be more tolerant of others and explain my ideas more carefully.
- I need to take time to try different things out before deciding on the best way forward.

Problem: not practising with props or music:
- example: you miss a cane that is thrown at you and it hits another performer
- possible impact on audience: messy, awkward performance
- avoiding the problem: practise with props/music as early as possible in the rehearsal process.

2 Example of possible outline production schedule based on musical theatre:
- response to stimulus: discussions, research, generating ideas for the plot and existing songs to be included
- development of ideas: creating a structure for the performance, creating a libretto, casting
- initial rehearsals: running through individual scenes; learning songs and creating dance routines.
- final rehearsals: linking scenes together; integrating musical and dance elements
- technical/dress/preview rehearsal: final run-through in performance space
- performance: performance day.

44. Performance skills and techniques

Individual responses. Here are some examples:

Communication
Expression: I used a mirror and video on my phone to practise my facial expressions so they were clear. My emotional reactions were understood by the audience, who clearly felt the tension of the moment.

Performance
Stillness: In the second scene I remained frozen so the focus shifted to two other characters. This was quite hard to do at first but in the course of rehearsals it became familiar and I was confident in my ability when it came to the performance.

Material
Music and songs: During the chorus of two songs I was able to harmonise. I practised this by singing my part with a recording on my phone, so I hit the high notes without any difficulty. The audience cheered at the end of the song and we knew we had communicated the sense of fun and celebration.

45. Sustaining performance

Individual responses. Two examples are given here.

Physical warm-up
1 Shake out tension from body – left hand, right hand, left leg, right leg, then whole body shake.

2 Stand centred (imagine string travelling up through body and out of top of head).

3 Stretches – reaching up to the ceiling with arms, reaching out to sides, slowly bending over from waist (vertebra by vertebra).

4 Quick group game – e.g. tag, stuck in the mud, grandmother's footsteps.

Vocal warm-up (if using voice)
1 Massage jaw and face.
2 Say tongue twisters.
3 Use scales – count one to eight, moving up and down scales.
4 Use songs – singing something everyone knows e.g. *I Like the Flowers*, a well-known pop song or song from a musical.

46. Preparing with others

Individual responses reflecting group and performance.

47. Performing with others

Individual responses. An example is given here:
I watched a scene from *The Curious Incident of the Dog in the Night-Time* by Frantic Assembly. The actors need to be aware of each other as well as the technical elements of the show. Their movements needed to be totally synchronised with the lighting and multimedia effects.

48. Communicating ideas

Individual responses that could consider the following points:
- Jets and Sharks perform aggressive gestures like punching their hands or holding weapons to show they are getting ready to fight. They sing in unison to show being in a gang.
- Anita is getting ready for her date with Bernardo after the rumble. She puts on tights, make-up and perfume during her lines, showing she is a mature lady.
- Maria is looking forward to seeing Tony. She sings of time moving slowly. She is wearing white and looks up to the sky innocently. She is different from Anita.

49. Reflecting on process

Individual responses should consider:
- the skills and techniques used in the rehearsal process
- your individual contribution
- how the piece was prepared in rehearsal
- how effective the rehearsals were in meeting the requirements of the brief.

50. Reflecting on the outcome

Individual responses can be about any professional performance or extract. Your considerations could include the:
- skills and techniques of performers and designers
- use of the performance space and props
- overall theme
- impact on you as the audience.

51. Improving process and the outcome

Individual responses. An example is given here:
The recording of the performance highlighted that I need to be more confident with my vocal delivery. There were times when I sounded really quiet and mumbling in comparison with the others, and I think that was me struggling to remember the lines. I tried not to show it physically, but I didn't think my accent was strong and that affected my projection and clarity. I will practise more on my vocal technique in future by using mouth and face exercises such as breathing, projection and tongue twisters. I'll also make sure I do proper warm-ups before rehearsal and performance, and practise my lines until I am fully confident.

52. Your Component 3 set task

Information reflecting the BTEC Tech Award Performing Arts Sample Assessment Material and Mark Scheme on the Pearson website.

53. Responding to a brief

Individual responses. The example below is one way of considering key stages when organising the development process. The information could be further used to help inform a rehearsal schedule and deadline calendar. Notes of the below should be made in skills and ideas logs.

- **Ideas and brainstorming.** Choose a target audience and purpose. Explore and investigate the stimulus/theme/ideas.
- **Share investigations** of the stimulus/theme and thoughts on existing performance material (other performance work in your preferred style, or with the same theme as the task). Make proposals and practical experiments.
- **Make first decisions** relating to content, focus, style, role(s), performance space/props, script/score/music/stage directions. Make sure all elements of the task are considered, and everyone has an opportunity to contribute ideas. Learn material.
- **Development of structure and content of piece**, minute by minute or scene by scene. Learn material.
- **Development.** Learn material. Group meeting about work in progress. Decisions about performance space and props finalised (if appropriate). Ensure individual contribution to the content of the work. Practise.
- **Finalising work, rehearsals and run-through** (initial rehearsals, final rehearsals, technical/dress/preview rehearsal). Evaluate any changes to be made before the workshop performance. Make sure of performance time – how long, and implications on the rehearsal schedule. Practise.
- **Workshop performance.** Following which, make notes in relation to the evaluation report.
- **Group discussion.** Evaluate performance. Make notes in relation to the evaluation report.
- **Complete final write-up** of notes for ideas and skills logs and in relation to the evaluation report.
- **Time management skills overall:** Some examples that help ensure deadlines are met:
  - Make sure your calendar/diary is up to date, setting aside time to complete tasks, rehearsals, individual practice and line-learning.
  - Create a realistic schedule and ensure you follow it.
  - Know exactly what you need to do (so you don't waste time on irrelevant tasks).

54. Ideas log notes 1

Individual responses. Consider whether you:
- used clear, focused bullet points
- noted the target audience and purpose
- noted the initial exploration and investigation in response to the requirements of the brief
- showed your understanding of the brief and how your ideas for performance took the brief into consideration
- noted what you did and why you did it to demonstrate clear objectives for development of the work.

55. Ideas log notes 2

Individual responses. Consider whether you noted your individual contribution to:
- how the work of others influenced your ideas
- the resources needed for development and performance
- the schedule to meet the performance date.

56. Skills log notes 1

Individual responses. Consider whether you made clear bullet points that noted:
- specific details about your target audience, and how your selection of skills and techniques were appropriate to engage them

- your role(s) in performance and the characteristics that led to your selection of skills and techniques
- how the skills and techniques chosen communicated your ideas and character to the target audience.

57. Skills log notes 2

Individual responses. Consider whether you noted:
- specific details about the skills and techniques you developed, and why
- the investigations you made to develop your skills, and how you refined your skills and techniques
- how you developed skills and techniques in relation to working with other performers
- how your individual contribution in rehearsals developed the group's skills and techniques to meet the brief and engage the target audience
- the specific ways that the work of others influenced the development of skills and techniques and how they were included in your performance.

58–69. Acting, dance and musical theatre ideas logs and skills logs

Individual responses, depending on the performance and selected ideas and skills.

70. Preparing and performing 1

Answer dependent on your last performance. Examples are given here.

Acting
- Mishap: I forgot my lines in the last section as another performer tripped up and made me laugh.
- How to avoid: I could develop my focus and concentration, and maybe add in some more rehearsals of lines.

Dance
- Mishap: I slipped in the jumping section. I was putting in much more effort than I usually do and I lost my footing.
- How to avoid: I could put more effort into rehearsals so that the adrenalin of performance doesn't take me by surprise.

Musical theatre
- Mishap: I forgot the tune to a song because it was only the third time I had used the backing track, and it was different to singing along with the singer.
- How to avoid: I could introduce the backing tracks earlier in the rehearsal process to get more used to them.

71. Preparing and performing 2

Individual responses. A checklist for a workshop performance might include the following:
- solo warm-up
- group warm-up and focus exercise
- prepare for performance: set performance space and props
- communicate with other performers and stage management/ teacher to meet curtain-up/start time
- focus and breathing exercises
- channel nerves and adrenalin into energised performance
- in performance: be in the moment
- enjoy the experience of sharing our work with an audience.

72. Workshop performance debrief

Individual responses based on the performance chosen.

73–78. Acting, dance and musical theatre evaluation

Individual responses based on the performance ideas and areas for development.